God's Promises Start with a Problem

How God Uses Problems to Manifest His Glory

Os Hillman

ASLAN GROUP
PUBLISHING

Aslan Group Publishing
Cumming, GA USA

God's Promises Start with a Problem: How God Uses Problems to Manifest His Glory
Os Hillman

ISBN: 978-1-888582-35-2 (e-book)
ISBN: 978-1-888582-36-9 print

ISBN 978-0-13-601970-1

9780136019701

Printed in the United States of America

Table of Contents

Chapter

Page

Acknowledgement

It had been two years since my last book. Strange, but I had no topic of interest to write about. Usually God drops into my spirit something that burns in my soul that must come out.

In 2004 I was interviewed by the New York Times. They were doing a story on faith in the workplace. They asked for my advice and asked me if there was a person's story they could build their article around. It was going to be an insert in the Sunday paper. I gave them a recommendation that they ended up using.

After three interviews they called me and said, "Our writers would like to know what is the difference between a Christian in the workplace and a non-Christian? I explained to them I thought there were four attributes of a Christian in the workplace:

1) *Excellence* – We are to do our work with excellence. Daniel and his three friends did their work ten times better than anyone else.
2) *Integrity* – We are to do our work with integrity. David says in Psalm 51, that God desires truth in the inward parts.
3) *Service* – Jesus said if we want to be great, we must serve others.
4) *Miracles* – Acts 5:12 says the apostles did many miraculous signs in the public colonnade.

In 2024 I felt led to create a website based on Acts 5:12. The website features stories of miracles in the marketplace. www.The512Project.com A few months later I did a personal study on miracles in the Bible. They all had a common theme: it seemed every miracle had a problem attached to it.

Then, in March of 2025 I had a telephone call with my spiritual father in the marketplace, Gunnar Olson. Gunnar lives in Sweden and we often share what God is saying to us during those calls. The topic that day seem to follow the pattern of miracles in the marketplace. But during our conversation Gunnar made a statement that screamed in my spirit: "Promises Start with a Problem."

He expounded on that statement for the next several minutes. What Gunnar was actually saying was **God's promises usually start with a problem that leads to a miracle.**
I knew immediately that was the book I was to write. And I was to share a personal story of a miracle in the marketplace followed by a Biblical example on that same theme. Each chapter would have a different theme. And each story would be summarized with the Promise, the Problem and the Miracle.

Thankyou Gunnar for being the catalyst to get me to write this book.

I pray this book will encourage you to see God's problems as a miracle in the making.

Introduction: God's Promises Start with a Problem

The Bible is a tapestry of 66 books filled with divine encounters, human crises, and the ongoing battle between good and evil in the affairs of mankind. It is a love story woven with threads of triumph and tragedy, where miraculous victories occur when God's children choose to trust and obey Him.

At its core, the Bible tells of God's ultimate promise: to establish a perfect union with humanity—a world where man would live in harmony with God, exercising dominion over all creation as His sons and daughters. This was God's vision for mankind.

But with every promise comes a challenge. The first problem arose in the Garden of Eden when humanity disobeyed God, and sin entered the world. This act of disobedience disrupted the divine order, plunging all creation into brokenness and separation from God.

Yet, none of this caught God by surprise. Long before the foundations of the earth were laid, God had already conceived a plan of redemption. As Revelation 13:8 declares,

"All who dwell on the earth will worship him, whose names have not been written in the Book of Life of the Lamb slain from the foundation of the world."

The fall of Adam and Eve marked the beginning of humanity's struggle with sin, but it also set the stage for the greatest rescue mission in history. God's secret plan of redemption unfolded in the fullness of time when He sent His only Son, Jesus Christ, to seek and save the lost. As Luke 19:10 affirms,

"For the Son of Man has come to seek and to save that which was lost."

What began as humanity's greatest problem became the doorway to God's greatest miracle. Through Christ's death and resurrection, the promise of eternal life and restored relationship with God was made available to all who believe.

Every one of us desires a life of purpose and fulfillment. Yet, the journey to realizing God's promises is rarely without obstacles. From the pages of Scripture to the lives of people today, there is a common thread: Promises Often Begin with Problems.

The Bible is filled with stories of men and women who clung to God's promises while navigating impossible odds. Joseph endured betrayal and imprisonment before stepping into his destiny as a ruler in Egypt. Moses faced fear and rejection before leading Israel to freedom. And Esther risked her life to save her people, holding fast to her faith when all seemed lost.

These stories are not just ancient tales; they are timeless truths. They remind us that our problems are not the end but the beginning of something greater. They are the crucible where God refines us, strengthens us, and prepares us to walk into His promises.

In this book, you'll discover the powerful intersections of faith, perseverance, and God's miracles. Alongside the biblical accounts, you'll hear real-life stories of individuals who faced overwhelming challenges yet trusted God to fulfill the visions He placed in their hearts. Their journeys mirror the ancient truths, proving that the same God who worked in the past is working in our lives today. Each chapter has a modern-day story combined with a biblical story on the same theme. At the end of each chapter, we summarize the Promise, the Problem and the Miracle that took place in the story.

Are you facing a problem that feels insurmountable? Take heart. This book is for you. Together, we'll uncover how problems are the starting point of God's promises—and how every obstacle is an opportunity for His miracle-working power.

In the chapters that follow, we will explore how God's promises often emerge from life's greatest challenges. Through the stories of biblical figures and real-life testimonies, you'll discover that every problem is an opportunity for God to reveal His power, purpose, and faithfulness.

Chapter 1 - Is God in Control?

Over the last 30 years, I've traveled extensively, speaking to groups worldwide. I often open meetings with this question: "Is God in control?"

Without fail, hands shoot up in unanimous agreement. At that point, I say, "You're all wrong! Let me explain."

Yes, God is omnipotent and omnipresent, but one thing He gave humanity is free will. Each of us makes choices daily—whether to attend a meeting, go grocery shopping, or take a particular course of action. God didn't create us as robots. Free will is both a gift and a responsibility, and it has consequences. Much of the pain and suffering in the world stems from humanity's free will because God does not override it. He entrusted us with the stewardship of earth, starting with Adam and Eve in the Garden of Eden. But sin entered the world, disrupting the perfect harmony between God and humanity.

In John 12:31, Jesus refers to Satan as "the ruler of this world." Yet, in Psalm 8:5-6, we read, "You have made humankind a little lower than the angels and crowned them with glory and honor. You made them rulers over the works of Your hands; You put everything under their feet." At first glance, these scriptures seem contradictory. However, they reflect a larger truth: a spiritual war rages between humanity and the enemy.

God has given us the authority to represent His kingdom on earth, while Satan seeks to rule. This is the war taking place on planet earth. But here's the balance: though we live in this tension, God remains sovereign, and He has delegated responsibility to us. It's a lot like the concept of the Power of Attorney. He has given us a spiritual form of Power of Attorney while on earth. This understanding has profound implications for our work and daily lives.

Reclaiming What Was Lost

Luke 19:10 tells us, "The Son of Man came to seek and to save what was lost." Jesus didn't come only to save souls but also to reclaim the fullness of creation that sin had corrupted. He entrusted His disciples—and by extension, us—with "the keys of the Kingdom" (Matthew 16:19) to carry out His purposes on Earth.

Jesus empowered His followers with authority, saying in John 14:12, "Whoever believes in me will do the works I have been doing, and they will do even greater things than these." The Holy Spirit enables us to bind and loose in heaven and on earth, to walk in authority, and to advance God's kingdom in tangible ways. When Jesus prayed, "Your kingdom come, Your will be done on Earth as it is in heaven", He revealed our role in bringing heaven's reality to earth.

This realization is both humbling and empowering. We are co-laborers with God, and our prayers are crucial. Have you ever been awakened in the middle of the night with a burden to pray? Many people have. Why does this happen? Because God seeks to fulfill His will on earth through us. He has delegated authority to humanity, and prayer is often the means through which His purposes are accomplished.

Speaking with Authority

Consider the story of Moses in the wilderness. God commanded him to speak to the rock to bring forth water. Yet Moses, in frustration, struck the rock instead. Despite his disobedience, water still flowed. This story reminds us that God calls us to use our authority wisely.

Jesus modeled this throughout His ministry. When confronting demons, He issued simple commands: "Come out!" He spoke directly to the storm: "Peace, be still!" His prayers were often declarations of authority. He took authority over the spiritual and physical realm.

I experienced this principle firsthand early in my ministry. When my first book was published, I was required to purchase 1,000 copies. Months later, I still had stacks of unsold books in my basement. One Saturday morning, I felt impressed to pray over those books. I went downstairs and declared, "In the name of Jesus, leave this basement and be a blessing to someone who needs these books!"

That afternoon, I received an unexpected phone call from a ministry in Dallas, Texas, ordering 300 books—a $3,000 order! I had no prior relationship with this organization. It was a powerful reminder that God calls us to pray boldly and strategically. That does not mean God is a genie to respond to our every whim and we can speak to any situation to change that situation. It means we are to listen to the Holy Spirit to know what He wants to do in that situation at that time.

Standing in Authority

In Mark 11:23, Jesus said, "Truly I tell you, if anyone says to this mountain, 'Go, throw yourself into the sea,' and does not doubt in their heart but believes what they say will happen, it will be done for them."

What mountains are standing in your way? Whether it's a workplace challenge, a strained relationship, or a personal obstacle, God has empowered you to pray with authority. Romans 8:19 declares, "The creation waits in eager expectation for the children of God to be revealed." This verse speaks to our potential to mature in faith and partner with God to bring about His purposes.

Consider Jacob's story. God gave him a divine strategy to leave his controlling uncle Laban and start his own business. Similarly, Deuteronomy 8:18 reminds us that God gives us the ability to create wealth to establish His covenant. This truth applies to our work lives as well. God desires to bless and guide us, giving us creativity, wisdom, and strategies to overcome challenges and fulfill His calling.

Partnering with God

Prayer is central to this partnership. It's not just about asking for blessings but also about listening for God's direction. Ask Him, "What's on Your heart, Lord? What would You have me do?" He has entrusted us with His authority to enforce His covenant promises and manifest His kingdom on Earth.

As Matthew 16:19 reminds us, God has given us the keys of the Kingdom, enabling us to bind and loose on earth as it is in heaven. And as Psalm 115:16 states, "The highest heavens belong to the Lord, but the earth He has given to mankind."

Our mission is clear: to bring heaven to earth by living in alignment with God's purposes, walking in faith, and exercising the authority He has entrusted to us. And to destroy the works of the devil, just as Jesus did.

Summary

- **Promise**: God gave humanity free will and delegated His authority to enforce His covenant promises.

- **Problem**: Free will allows sin and human choices to affect the world.

- **Miracle**: Through the Holy Spirit, God empowers us to make right choices and fulfill His purposes by using our God-given authority.

Let us embrace our role as co-laborers with Christ, living boldly and intentionally to see His kingdom come and His will be done on earth as it is in heaven.

Chapter 2 - Manifesting God's Power in Our Calling

One of the early lessons I learned from my mentor, J. Gunnar Olson, founder of the International Christian Chamber of Commerce, is that all Christ-followers should be manifesting the presence of God in their work. When we look at the story of Moses, God's presence is evident in a profound way. At the burning bush, God told Moses, "Take off your shoes, for you are on holy ground." This was out in the desert, where Moses was shepherding dirty sheep. What made that ground holy? It was the presence of God.

God engaged Moses in a life-changing conversation. He asked, "What is that in your hand?" Moses replied, "It's my staff." The staff symbolized Moses' vocation. God then said, "I will perform miracles through your staff and deliver a people through it." God used Moses to manifest His presence, deliver the Israelites from slavery, and demonstrate His power to Egypt. In the same way, God calls us to manifest His presence in our work and fulfill our calling.

A New Testament Parallel

In Acts 5, we see how the disciples, filled with the Holy Spirit, performed miraculous signs in public. Their actions displayed God's manifest presence for all to see. Similarly, the Apostle Paul told the Corinthians, "My preaching and teaching are not with persuasive words, but by the power of God working in me." Paul recognized that his knowledge alone could not convince people; only God's manifest presence could.

Paul's ministry was filled with moments where God's power was evident. People were healed, and miraculous acts occurred. These events remind us that God's power is still at work today, and His Word remains unchanging. We are called to tap into God's power and presence in our calling.

Understanding that all of life is spiritual has profound implications for how we approach work. Unfortunately, Os Guinness, in his book, The Call, tells us that since 300 AD, many Christians have been taught that work is less spiritual, a second-class activity. That is called the Catholic Distortion. But Colossians 3:23–24 says, "Whatever you do, do it unto the Lord. It is the Lord Christ you are serving, and therein lies your inheritance."

Jesus Himself exemplified the value of work. For most of His life, He was known as a carpenter, not as the Messiah. His work was marked by excellence, service, integrity and miracles—qualities we too should strive for in our work. When we act this way, we reflect God in our lives.

Four Distinctive Marks of a Christian in the Workplace

During an interview years ago with *The New York Times*, I was asked, "What makes a Christian different in the workplace?" After prayerful consideration, I identified four key areas:

1. **Excellence**: In Daniel 1, Daniel and his friends did their work ten times better than anyone else.
2. **Integrity**: Psalm 51 says, "God desires truth in the inward parts." We should be the same person in private as we are in public.
3. **Servanthood**: Jesus said, "If you want to be great, be the servant of all."
4. **Miracles**: Christians are called to express the life and power of Christ in their work life as modeled in Acts 5:12. I have personally seen God move miraculously in work situations.

Gunnar Olson on Manifesting God's Presence

Gunnar Olson shared some profound insights on this topic in a discussion I had with him. He said, "There is a redemptive quality to the business and professional life that God wants to reveal before the Lord's return. Colossians 1:19–20 says, 'For it pleased the Father that in Him all the fullness should dwell, and by Him to reconcile all things to Himself.'"

Gunnar emphasized that God's reconciliation includes all aspects of life, including business. He posed a thought-provoking question: 'What does a reconciled business look like?' The answer lies in the presence and glory of God. Jesus demonstrated this supernatural dimension throughout His ministry, such as providing tax money from a fish."

Gunnar's yearning is for all Christians to walk in the supernatural as a normal part of their professional lives. He said, "Merging a walk through the Spirit with professional excellence is not easy, but it is our calling. God yearns for His presence to be manifested in the marketplace in a way specific to our time."

Gunnar also distinguished between God's manifest presence and His miraculous acts. While miracles are extraordinary, the consistent presence of God in our work brings transformation. Manifesting God's power in our calling requires us to live by faith, seek His presence, and invite Him into every aspect of our work.

Conclusion

God's call to manifest His presence is as relevant today as it was for Moses, Paul, and the early disciples. As we embrace our calling, let us work with excellence, integrity, servanthood, and faith, trusting God to demonstrate His power through us. By doing so, we fulfill His purpose and bring His kingdom to earth.

Summary

Promise: *And Jesus came and spoke to them, saying, "All authority has been given to Me in heaven and on earth. Go therefore and make disciples of all the nations, baptizing them in the name of the Father and of the Son and of the Holy Spirit, teaching them to observe all things that I have commanded you; and lo, I am with you always, even to the end of the age." Amen. – Matthew 28:18-20*

Problem: There are many reasons we will experience problems in life. God calls us to appropriate His solutions to every problem.

Miracle: God calls us to use this authority to bind and loose in heaven and on earth to solve problems.

Chapter 3 - "Forgive the Debt!"

I was on the phone with my attorney, explaining a difficult decision I had just made: I was going to forgive a $140,000 debt owed by one of my ad agency's clients. This client had been our largest, accounting for 80% of our business. Despite our best efforts to resolve a problem with a project we had done for him, he remained dissatisfied. He not only refused to pay the bill, he fired us as his ad agency.

The situation had escalated to a lawsuit. It was heartbreaking because we had poured years of effort into his success. Through our innovative advertising strategies, we had grown his business from $10 million to over $25 million annually. Our work even won prestigious national and international awards. But now, it seemed that none of that mattered.

At the time, my life was already in turmoil. My wife had told me she wanted a divorce, and I had just lost $500,000 in a Bernie Madoff-style scam. To add insult to injury, this lawsuit was hanging over my head. The weight of it all felt unbearable.

During this season, God brought a man into my life—a mentor who felt like a "John the Baptist" figure. He spoke hard truths and gave wise counsel. One day, he told me, "You need to forgive your client. You still have a part in this situation to own."

I resisted his advice. My mind raced with thoughts of fairness and justice. "This isn't fair!" I cried out. I believed we were only 10% at fault in this situation, and we had done everything possible to make it right. Yet, my mentor was unwavering. He urged me to trust God and take a leap of faith.

Reluctantly, I decided to act. I called my attorney and informed him to cancel the lawsuit. I pondered the following scripture:

"You have heard that it was said, 'You shall love your neighbor and hate your enemy.' But I say to you, love your enemies, bless those who curse you, do good to those who hate you, and pray for those who spitefully use you and persecute you, that you may be sons of your Father in heaven; for He makes His sun rise on the evil and on the good, and sends rain on the just and on the unjust. For if you love those who love you, what reward have you? Do not even the tax collectors do the same? And if you greet your brethren only, what do you do more than others? Do not even the tax collectors do so? Therefore you shall be perfect, just as your Father in heaven is perfect." - Matthew 5:44-48

"You can't do this," he argued. "Your client has countersued you. Dropping the case will leave you completely exposed!"

"Forgive the suit," I said firmly.

"You're crazy!"

Despite his protests, I instructed my attorney to notify the client that we were dropping the lawsuit. My mentor also encouraged me to personally reach out to my client and ask for his forgiveness.

I called my client's secretary, whom I had known for years, and dictated my message word for word she was to share with my client:

"I have seen my error in this recent project and wrongfully sued you. I ask for your forgiveness for my part in this. I am dropping my lawsuit."

To my surprise, the secretary began to cry. Later that day, my client called. He said he had received my message, accepted my apology, and forgave me. Shortly after, my attorney informed me that the countersuit had also been dropped.

We later met for lunch to clear the air. The meeting was cordial, but my client refused to take any responsibility for the situation and still refused to pay the $140,000 he owed. On top of that, I had over $40,000 in vendor costs tied to the project that I had to absorb. It would take me five years to pay off the debt while facing other financial and personal challenges.

This marked the beginning of a seven-year season of adversity. During this time, a spiritual father in the marketplace told me I had a "Joseph Calling" on my life—a calling to be both a spiritual and physical provider to others. But he warned me that fulfilling this calling would require pressing into God with my whole heart.

In the seventh year, during the same month my adversity began, God brought an unexpected breakthrough. I was able to sell a piece of property I had purchased for $95,000 for $600,000. This allowed me to pay off all my debts and even purchase a home with cash.

Through this experience, I learned that God's answers don't always come quickly, but His timing is perfect. When we trust Him and walk in obedience, He fulfills His purposes in our lives—even through seasons of famine.

Fast forward 5 years. That life-changing period led me to share my experiences through a daily devotional called Today God Is First that would be read in 105 countries. Thirty years later I would write 26 books and train leaders in 26 countries. God truly turned my Valley of Achor (trouble) Hosea 2:15, into a door of hope for me and hundreds of thousands of others around the world.

God's promises often start with a problem. Consider the problem you face as an opportunity to manifest God's solution.

Joseph experienced seven years of plenty and seven years of famine.

Summary

Promise: Forgive your enemies. God will provide all your needs.

Problem: Client refuses to pay his bill. Fires me as their client.

Miracle: God provides 6x return on a property to restore all finances and become debt free.

What test is God giving you today? Whatever it is, I pray you will trust Him for the outcome.

The Parable of the Unforgiving Servant

The following story in the scriptures gives us a marketplace case study of forgiveness. It is probably a story of what takes place in marketplaces around the world every day. Let's read the account in Matthew 18:21-35.

> *Then Peter came to Him and said, "Lord, how often shall my brother sin against me, and I forgive him? Up to seven times?"*
>
> *Jesus said to him, "I do not say to you, up to seven times, but up to seventy times seven. Therefore, the kingdom of heaven is like a certain king who wanted to settle accounts with his servants. And when he had begun to settle accounts, one was brought to him*

who owed him ten thousand talents. But as he was not able to pay, his master commanded that he be sold, with his wife and children and all that he had, and that payment be made. The servant therefore fell down before him, saying, 'Master, have patience with me, and I will pay you all.' Then the master of that servant was moved with compassion, released him, and forgave him the debt.

"But that servant went out and found one of his fellow servants who owed him a hundred denarii; and he laid hands on him and took him by the throat, saying, 'Pay me what you owe!' So his fellow servant fell down at his feet and begged him, saying, 'Have patience with me, and I will pay you all.' And he would not, but went and threw him into prison till he should pay the debt. So when his fellow servants saw what had been done, they were very grieved, and came and told their master all that had been done. Then his master, after he had called him, said to him, 'You wicked servant! I forgave you all that debt because you begged me. Should you not also have had compassion on your fellow servant, just as I had pity on you?' And his master was angry, and delivered him to the torturers until he should pay all that was due to him.

"So My heavenly Father also will do to you if each of you, from his heart, does not forgive his brother his trespasses."

Forgiveness is more for the person holding unforgiveness than the one who is the victim to unforgiveness. Unforgiveness creates an emotional jailcell and has proven to result in physical manifestations of arthritis and other diseases. If you are holding unforgiveness towards another make a decision today to forgive your offender so that you can be free to fulfill God's purposes for you.

The Parable of the Unforgiving Servant

In the marketplace, forgiveness often seems like a foreign concept. Yet, as followers of Christ, we are called to embody it in our dealings. The story of the Unforgiving Servant in Matthew 18:21-35 offers a vivid case study that illustrates the power and necessity of forgiveness in every area of life, including the workplace. Let us delve into this scripture to glean its profound lessons.

The Story

Peter approached Jesus with a question many of us may ponder: "Lord, how often shall my brother sin against me, and I forgive him? Up to seven times?" (Matthew 18:21). Peter likely thought he was being generous, as Jewish tradition often taught forgiving someone up to three times. But Jesus' reply shattered any notion of limited forgiveness: "I do not say to you, up to seven times, but up to seventy times seven" - Matthew 18:22

In other words, forgiveness should be limitless. Jesus then illustrated His point with a parable:

A king decided to settle accounts with his servants. One servant owed him an astronomical debt of ten thousand talents—a sum so large it was impossible to repay. When the servant could not pay, the king ordered that he, his family, and all his possessions be sold to settle the debt. Desperate, the servant fell before the king and pleaded for patience, promising to pay everything. Moved with compassion, the king forgave the debt entirely.

However, this same servant went out and confronted a fellow servant who owed him a much smaller amount—just a hundred denarii. Grabbing him by the throat, he demanded repayment. The fellow servant begged for patience, just as the first servant had done, but the unforgiving servant refused. He had his fellow servant thrown into prison until the debt was repaid.

When other servants witnessed this injustice, they reported it to the king. Enraged, the king called the unforgiving servant and said, "You wicked servant! I forgave you all that debt because you begged me. Should you not also have had compassion on your fellow servant, just as I had pity on you?" The king then delivered him to the torturers until he could repay the original debt. Jesus concluded with a sobering statement: "So My heavenly Father also will do to you if each of you, from his heart, does not forgive his brother his trespasses" - Matthew 18:35

Marketplace Implications

This parable is not just a story for Sunday school; it reflects the realities of life and business. Every day, people face situations that require forgiveness: a client who breaks a promise, a colleague who takes credit for your work, or a business partner who lets you down. These are moments when we must choose whether to extend grace or harbor resentment.

Forgiveness in the marketplace is crucial for several reasons:

1. **Freedom for the Forgiver**: Unforgiveness creates an emotional and spiritual prison. Medical research has linked chronic resentment to physical ailments such as arthritis, high blood pressure, and heart disease. Forgiveness, on the other hand, releases the burden and fosters healing.

2. **Reflecting God's Grace**: Just as the king forgave the servant's insurmountable debt, we are called to forgive others as God has forgiven us. Our ability to forgive reflects our understanding and gratitude for the grace we have received.

3. **Restoring Relationships**: The marketplace thrives on trust and collaboration. Unforgiveness erodes these foundations, while forgiveness can mend and strengthen them.

A Call to Action

Take a moment to reflect. Are you holding onto unforgiveness toward someone in your life? Perhaps it's a business partner, a coworker, or even a family member. Holding onto resentment does more harm to you than to the other person. It chains you to the past and hinders your ability to move forward.

Make a decision today to forgive. This does not mean excusing wrongdoing or minimizing the hurt you've experienced. Forgiveness is a choice to release the offender into God's hands and free yourself from the weight of bitterness. It's a step of faith that aligns your heart with God's purposes for your life.

"If your enemy is hungry, give him bread to eat; And if he is thirsty, give him water to drink; For in doing so, you will heap coals of fire upon his head, and the LORD will reward you." - Proverbs 25:21-22

Conclusion

The Parable of the Unforgiving Servant is a reminder that forgiveness is not optional for those who follow Christ. It's a command that brings freedom, healing, and restoration. In the marketplace and beyond, let us strive to emulate the king in the story, extending the same grace to others that we have received from our heavenly Father. By doing so, we fulfill God's calling and position ourselves to walk in His blessings.

Summary

Promise: Forgive, then you will be forgiven. If not, you will not be forgiven.

Problem: Servant failed to extend grace to the one who was indebted to him.

Miracle: Unfortunately, the miracle was not extended to the servant after refusing to forgive.

It was painful to forgive the man who took advantage of me and refused to own his indiscretion that impacted me for almost 7 years. However, I was emotionally free during that time and believe I received a measure of grace during that season and was able to rejoice when God restored my finances through a supernatural sale of a piece of property.

Chapter 4 - Using Your Authority for Breakthrough

My spiritual father in the marketplace is J. Gunnar Olson. Several years ago, he wrote a book called Business Unlimited. In this book he shares a powerful story of using his spiritual authority to get a breakthrough for a business owner in his area.

"One of my friends had a company that manufactured pine products, predominantly as a subcontractor to the furniture industry. He was only just making ends meet. There was no profit at all. And so when he phoned me, he was desperate. Something had to change, or he would have to give up.

When I went over to see him, I took a financial expert with me, a banker. This man was an expert in corporate analysis, and he could always pinpoint the weak spots in a business. A whole day was spent thoroughly investigating the production process and the entire budget, and the only weakness we found was a high level of raw material waste. In the production process, the knots of the branches were cut out and only the remaining wood was used to produce perfect pine products. Twenty-seven percent of the raw material was wasted. Therefore, we concluded that if this waste could be used, it would make the company profitable.

"What are you doing with this waste?" I asked. "We use it to heat the place," my friend replied.

"Do you have anything left after you have heated the factory?" I felt prompted to ask. "Do I have anything left?" he laughed. "I have a whole mountain left!"

As soon as he said "mountain," I felt something trigger in my spirit, and I knew that this was what the Holy Spirit had been waiting for.

"Let's go and look at it," I suggested.

He took us across the large building, and I realized that he had not been exaggerating when he referred to the waste wood as a mountain. The pile was about the height of a house, and it was simply scrap. As we gazed at this "mountain" I was overcome with a new boldness.

"This mountain is the solution to your problems," I announced.

Several workers had shown a keen interest in our little group and wondered what we were doing. Ignoring their puzzled expressions, I continued as I felt instructed by the Holy Spirit and explained we were going to pray. Now, we really had everyone's attention. All eyes were focused on us as we stood by the mountain of wood on the factory floor.

"We're going to do something unusual, but you carry on," I suggested. Few, if any, of the folk on the factory floor were believers, and so our behavior must have seemed strange to say the least. By now I had started praying, and I shouted at the top of my voice: "In the name of the Lord Jesus Christ, I command this mountain of waste wood to heave itself up and become a product! Thank you, Lord, amen!"

Although my friend and the banker were Christians, they were clearly embarrassed by my extreme behavior. Swedes are naturally reserved people, and my shouting had shocked them. They had probably expected me to pray quietly and certainly not to bellow out so loudly in front of the workers. In fact, as soon as I had finished praying, I suddenly felt quite ridiculous. Making some excuse, we left quickly. I thought I had gone completely over the top and upset everyone. Moreover, I must have looked like an idiot. I really felt ridiculous and couldn't wait to get away.

Two weeks later the owner of the factory telephoned me. Something extraordinary had happened and he thought I should be the first to know. Someone from Norway had called him and asked if he could make the center piece of kitchen cabinet doors. His request had been remarkable because he did not want the good part of the wood, but only the knots and eyes of branches. The mountain was moving at last. By the end of that year the company had an excellent profit.

Once more I was learning. The boldness I had experienced was because I knew I was standing in a position of authority in Jesus. This was totally different to those intimate times of prayer. I had been standing under a heavenly mandate given by God through the Holy Spirit. Since then, we have had many similar experiences at Alfapac when we have had to take our authority as believers and act in the name of Jesus in prayer to see results."[1]

Summary:

Promise: *"You will also declare a thing, and it will be established for you; So light will shine on your ways." – Job 22:28*

Problem: Business owner could not make a profit in his business.

Miracle: Gunnar felt led by the Holy Spirit to speak to the mountain of wasted wood to be sold. Company called to buy the knotted wood only, which allowed the company to make a profit.

Speak to Your Mountain: The Power of Prophetic Decrees

There are moments in life when your mountain will not move until you speak to it. Jesus made this radical statement in *Mark 11:23*: *"Truly I tell you, if anyone says to this mountain, 'Go, throw yourself into the sea,' and does not doubt in their heart but believes that what they say will happen, it will be done for them."*

Jesus didn't say *pray about the mountain*—He said *speak to it.* This wasn't just poetic language; He was teaching a spiritual principle. In the kingdom of God, faith often requires our participation. And in many cases, that participation begins with speaking.

Let's explore eight powerful biblical examples where men of God spoke to impossible situations—and saw divine breakthroughs as a result.

1. Jesus Speaks to the Fig Tree - (Mark 11:12–14, 20–24)

Jesus approaches a fig tree looking for fruit. When He finds none, He says, *"May no one ever eat fruit from you again."* By the next day, the fig tree is completely withered from the roots. His disciples are amazed. Jesus then turns the moment into a teaching on mountain-moving faith: *"Have faith in God... whoever says to this mountain... it will be done for them."*

Key Insight: Jesus models the power of speaking directly to fruitlessness—and expecting change.

2. Jesus Commands the Storm - (Mark 4:35–41)

In the middle of a violent storm, while His disciples panic, Jesus rises and speaks three words: *"Peace, be still!"* Immediately, the wind and waves obey. The natural world responds to His voice.

Key Insight: Even the chaos around you must yield when faith speaks with authority.

3. Joshua Commands the Sun to Stand Still - (Joshua 10:12–14)

In the heat of battle, Joshua boldly commands the sun and moon to hold their position: *"Sun, stand still over Gibeon!"* God honors his command, and time literally freezes. Scripture notes: *"There has never been a day like it before or since..."*

Key Insight: God will stop natural laws when His servants declare in alignment with His purposes.

4. Elijah Declares a Drought - (1 Kings 17:1)

Elijah stands before King Ahab and boldly declares, *"There shall be neither dew nor rain... except at my word."* For over three years, the skies remain closed—until Elijah speaks again.

Key Insight: A man walking in obedience can shape the climate—literally and spiritually—by his words.

5. Ezekiel Prophesies to Dry Bones - (Ezekiel 37:1–10)

God takes Ezekiel to a valley of dry bones and says, *"Prophesy to these bones..."* As Ezekiel speaks, the bones rattle, connect, are covered in flesh, and come to life as a mighty army.

Key Insight: Some dead things won't live again until *you* speak life over them.

6. Peter Speaks Healing to a Lame Man - (Acts 3:6–8)

At the temple gate, Peter declares to a lame man: *"In the name of Jesus Christ of Nazareth, rise up and walk!"* Instantly, the man jumps up, healed and whole.

Key Insight: Healing can be released by faith-filled words spoken in Jesus' name.

7. Jesus Calls Lazarus from the Grave - (John 11:43–44)

Jesus stands before the tomb of His friend and cries out: *"Lazarus, come forth!"* A man four days dead walks out of the grave alive.

Key Insight: Resurrection power is activated by the spoken word of faith.

8. Paul Commands a Demon to Leave - (Acts 16:18)

Annoyed by a spirit of divination harassing him, Paul finally turns and says: *"I command you in the name of Jesus Christ to come out of her!"* Immediately, the spirit leaves.

Key Insight: Spiritual opposition must flee when confronted by kingdom authority.

Patterns We Can Follow

Across all these examples, four common elements emerge:

1. **Authority** – They spoke with God-given or Spirit-led authority.
2. **Faith** – They believed their words would produce results.
3. **Obedience** – They often spoke because God prompted them to.

4. **Impact** – Something in the natural or spiritual realm *changed immediately*.

Your Words Matter

You were created in the image of a speaking God. The Bible opens with *"And God said..."* not once but repeatedly. God created by speaking, and He empowers us to do the same. Proverbs 18:21 says: *"Death and life are in the power of the tongue..."*

When you're facing a mountain—be it fear, sickness, lack, or injustice—you must do more than pray about it. You must speak to it.

Activation: Speaking to Your Mountain

Think of the mountain you are facing today. Now, speak to it:

- **To fear**: *"You have no hold on me. God has not given me a spirit of fear."*
- **To debt**: *"My God supplies all my needs. Debt, be removed!"*
- **To sickness**: *"By His stripes, I am healed!"*
- **To delay**: *"In Jesus' name, I call forth acceleration."*
- **To doubt**: *"I have the mind of Christ and sound judgment."*

Faith in Action

Faith that doesn't speak is faith that's still in hiding. Don't wait for your situation to change before you speak—speak so your situation will change.

Like Jesus, Joshua, Elijah, Peter, and Paul—you have been given authority to declare truth into darkness, chaos, and delay.

Your words can shift atmospheres, open doors, and release miracles.

Speak to your mountain. And watch it move.

Summary:

Promise: Jesus gave us the keys of the Kingdom to bind and loose on earth and in heaven. He told us to speak to our mountains to be removed.

Problem: There are many obstacles that get in our way. Use your authority to get breakthroughs.

Miracle: The above examples of miracles should build your faith as a Kingdom warrior in the marketplace.

Chapter 5: The Importance of Hearing God's Voice

Hearing God's voice is an essential aspect of the Christian walk. It's the foundation of a dynamic and fruitful relationship with Him. Recently, I had the privilege of interviewing Andy Mason, the founder of Heaven in Business, a marketplace ministry, and author of *Listen Up! Hearing God at Work*. We discussed the critical importance of hearing God's voice in our daily lives and work, and how it serves as a gateway to experiencing God's miracles and guidance.

Addressing Doubts About Hearing God's Voice

Many Christians struggle with the idea of hearing God's voice, often doubting that they hear Him at all. I asked Andy how he would respond to someone who claims they don't hear from God.

Andy's response was both encouraging and insightful: "John 10:27 tells us, 'My sheep hear my voice.' This is not optional; it's a truth Jesus declared. The issue is not whether God is speaking, but whether we recognize His voice. Often, people haven't been taught to discern what God's voice sounds like in their lives."

Andy shared a remarkable story from his book about Kevin, a devout atheist who inherited a struggling staffing company. Amid his business challenges, Kevin began hearing a voice in his head—one that provided specific, actionable guidance. As he followed this voice—firing a client here, making a strategic hire there—the business began to thrive. At first, Kevin didn't realize the voice was God's, but when his wife asked to visit Bethel Church for her birthday, Kevin found himself prompted by the same voice to go. During the service, as he reluctantly lifted his hands in worship as instructed by this internal voice, Kevin experienced a revelation: the voice guiding him was God's. This transformation not only changed his life but also his business, which continues to prosper under God's guidance.

This story illustrates that even those who don't yet believe can hear God's voice. How much more, then, should followers of Jesus expect to hear Him?

In environments like Bethel, where there's a culture of hearing from God, it's common to encounter people who share what they believe God is saying to them. For example, I was walking across a parking lot one day when a young man approached me. He asked, "Can you help me hear the voice of God?"

I replied, "Okay, tell me more. What do you mean by that?"

He explained, "I have these roommates who are always saying, 'God told me this' or 'God said that.' But I don't know what they mean. How do they hear God?"

I asked, "When they say that, did you ask them what they mean?"

He said, "Yeah, and they told me it's like a still, small voice—an internal, almost audible voice."

At that moment, the Holy Spirit quickened something in me. I asked him, "When you think, do you think in words, pictures, or sounds?"

He replied, "Oh, I'm an artist. I think in pictures." His passion was drawing comics, so his thought processes were naturally visual rather than verbal.

"Okay," I said, "Let's try something. The Bible says that God speaks and we listen, that He answers when we cry out to Him. His thoughts toward you are good and more numerous than the sand on the seashore. So let's align our hearts with that truth. I want you to take your pen and ask the Holy Spirit to show you how He sees you. Then, just draw whatever comes to mind."

I expected something simple, but what he drew stunned me. He sketched a cliff with an old-fashioned bomb—the kind with a burning fuse. A hand, coming down from heaven, was pouring water onto the fuse to extinguish it. Life was springing up all around the scene.

He explained, "That's me. I have a short fuse; I get angry easily. But Jesus comes in, pours out His love, and takes away the anger. What's left is life."

I looked at him and said, "You told me you couldn't hear God, but this—this is hearing God. Don't compare yourself to others. God speaks to you in the way you understand best. For you, it's through pictures."

God Speaks in Many Ways

Many of us hear God more than we realize, but we don't pause to listen. Sometimes, the harder we try, the more elusive His voice seems. I've heard countless people say they hear God most often in unexpected places, like the bathroom, when they're not consciously trying. A thought pops into their mind, seemingly out of nowhere. This is often how God speaks—unexpectedly and in ways we're not striving to manufacture.

Years ago, I was at a conference in New York City with about ten speakers. The event was poorly organized, and only 20 people showed up. Many of us were irritated, myself included. The organizer lamented that the event's failure would bankrupt her. As I sat there, frustrated, a thought popped into my head: "Give her $1,000."

I knew immediately that wasn't my thought. Left to my own reasoning, I wouldn't have come up with that. But I recognized it as God's prompting and obeyed.

This kind of moment reminds me of the story of Samuel. When Samuel first heard God's voice, he didn't recognize it and had to be instructed by his mentor, Eli the priest, to respond. Similarly, when an unexpected thought or impression comes, we should pause and ask, "Lord, is that You?"

A Practical Approach to Hearing God

Here are some key things to remember:

1. **Know that God speaks in ways unique to you.** Some people hear an internal voice; others see pictures, feel impressions, or even sense God's presence through actions.

2. **Be available and open.** God often speaks when we're not expecting it. Create moments of quiet and stillness to tune your heart to His voice.

3. **Test unexpected thoughts.** If a thought comes that's aligned with God's character and something you wouldn't naturally think of, it may very well be Him.

4. **Respond in faith.** Like Samuel, when you believe God is speaking, respond. Even if you're unsure, stepping out in faith strengthens your ability to discern His voice over time.

God's voice is more accessible than we often realize. The key is to trust that He desires to speak and to remain open to hearing Him in the way He chooses to communicate with you.

Foundations for Hearing God's Voice

Andy emphasized two foundational principles for discerning God's voice:

1. **Alignment with Scripture:** God's voice will never contradict His Word. The Bible is our ultimate guide and litmus test for everything we believe God is saying.

2. **Wise Counsel:** Proverbs teaches us that wisdom is found in the multitude of counselors. God often confirms His voice through trusted advisors and community.

In addition to these foundations, Andy outlined three practical questions to help discern whether something is from God:

1. Does It Release Life?

Jesus said in John 6:63, "My words are Spirit and they are life." When God speaks, His words bring clarity, energy, and conviction. Andy explained, "If something is from God, it will propel you forward with a sense of purpose and vitality. If it's not from God, it will often feel dull or lifeless."

2. Does It Bring Peace?

Colossians 3:15 says, "Let the peace of Christ rule in your hearts." Andy shared a personal example of being invited to join the board of a startup. While the opportunity aligned with his values and vision, and even moved him to tears with its potential, he felt an unshakable hesitation when it came time to commit. Despite having no logical reason, he chose to trust that lack of peace as God's guidance. Years later, he still doesn't know why it wasn't the right move, but he's confident he followed God's direction.

3. Is It Consistent with God's Character?

Discernment often involves recognizing the subtle difference between what is good and what is almost right. Andy explained that God's voice will always align with His character—marked by wisdom, love, and truth—even when it challenges us or doesn't make immediate sense.

Hearing God's voice is not enough; it requires a willingness to act. I shared my own experience of wanting to connect with a publisher to have a longterm publishing relationship. I received a letter from the president of a publishing company that I respected and felt would be a good publishing partner. I sat down to write them a letter but kept encountering an inexplicable check in my spirit. Months later, God orchestrated a meeting with the publisher that led to a relationship far more valuable than anything I could have arranged on my own. Sometimes, God's guidance doesn't make sense in the moment, but obedience always leads to His best for us.

Andy's experience shows that many people hear from God more than they realize. He explained, "People often dismiss God's voice, assuming it's their own thoughts. But the truth is, if you're a follower of Jesus, you already hear Him. It's about learning to recognize and respond."

Developing this skill requires time, intentionality, and practice. Spending time in God's Word, praying, and inviting the Holy Spirit to lead are all essential practices. The more we tune our hearts to Him, the more clearly we'll hear His voice.

Conclusion

Hearing God's voice is not reserved for a select few; it's a promise to all who follow Jesus. As Andy's stories demonstrate, God's voice brings life, peace, and purpose to every aspect of our lives. Whether in business, relationships, or daily decisions, learning to hear and obey God's voice positions us to experience His miracles and fulfill His plans for us. Let's cultivate the practice of listening and responding, knowing that God is always speaking to those who seek Him.

The stories we will hear about in this book often depend on the leader's ability and obedience to God's voice.

Summary:

Promise: *"My sheep hear My voice, and I know them, and they follow Me." – John 10:27*

Problem: Many people either fail to believe God speaks to them or that don't know how to recognize His voice.

Miracle: When you discover that God actually does speak to you, your life is never the same. You begin to trust His voice and get breakthroughs in your life.

How King David Learned to Hear God to Win Battles

The Bible provides many examples of men and women who learned to hear God's voice and follow His direction. One of the most striking examples is King David, who relied on God for guidance, especially during times of battle. David's story demonstrates the importance of waiting on God's timing, listening for His voice, and trusting His strategy, even when it might not align with human logic.

David was known as a man after God's own heart. This wasn't because he was perfect—he wasn't—but because he sought God earnestly and depended on Him for guidance. One remarkable example is found in 2 Samuel 5:22-25.

David faced the Philistines, a persistent enemy of Israel. Instead of relying solely on his military experience or strategies from previous victories, David inquired of the Lord. God gave him specific instructions for this battle:

"Do not go straight up, but circle around behind them and attack them in front of the poplar trees. As soon as you hear the sound of marching in the tops of the poplar trees, move quickly, because that will mean the Lord has gone out in front of you to strike the Philistine army" (2 Samuel 5:23-24, NIV).

David obeyed and waited for the sign—the sound of marching in the trees. Only then did he move forward, and the result was a decisive victory.

Key Lessons from David's Example

1. **Seek God's Guidance First**
   Before taking any action, David asked God what he should do. This highlights the importance of consulting God, especially in critical decisions. Hearing from God starts with an intentional act of seeking His direction through prayer and meditation on His Word.

2. **God's Strategies Are Unique**
   David didn't assume that previous strategies would work again. In a prior battle with the Philistines, God instructed him to attack directly, but this time, the strategy was different. God's guidance is tailored to specific situations, reminding us not to lean on our understanding but to trust His unique plan for each challenge.

3. **Wait for God's Timing**
   The instruction to wait until hearing the sound of marching in the trees required patience and faith. Acting prematurely could have led to disaster. Similarly, hearing God often requires waiting on His perfect timing, even when circumstances seem urgent.

4. **God Goes Before Us**
   The sound of marching symbolized that God's angelic forces were moving ahead of David's army. This reassured David that the battle belonged to the Lord. When we hear and follow God's voice, we can have confidence that He is working on our behalf, even in unseen realms.

Cultivating a Listening Ear

David's ability to hear God was cultivated through a deep relationship with Him. As a shepherd, David spent hours in solitude, worshiping, and meditating on God's greatness. This intimacy laid the foundation for recognizing God's voice in times of crisis.

Here are practical ways to cultivate a listening ear like David:

- **Spend Time in God's Presence:** Regular prayer and worship help us become attuned to His voice.
- **Study the Scriptures:** God's written Word is His primary way of speaking to us.
- **Be Sensitive to the Holy Spirit:** The Spirit often guides us with promptings, impressions, or a sense of peace.
- **Practice Obedience:** The more we obey God's voice, the clearer His guidance becomes in our lives.

Conclusion

King David's victories were not just the result of his skill or courage but his reliance on God's voice. By seeking God's guidance, trusting His strategies, and waiting for His timing, David experienced success and brought glory to God.

In our own lives, we can learn to hear God by prioritizing our relationship with Him, seeking His direction in every decision, and stepping out in faith when He speaks. Just as David heard the sound of marching in the trees, we too can hear God's voice guiding us to victory in the battles we face.

Summary:

Promise: *"Whether you turn to the right or to the left, your ears will hear a voice behind you, saying, 'This is the way; walk in it.'" – Isaiah 31:21*

Problem: David needed God's strategy to defeat his enemies.

Miracle: David waited on God to reveal strategy and timing to defeat his enemies.

Chapter 6 - 5 Points

I first met Emeka Nywankpa in 1998 at the Global Conference on World Evangelism through Gunnar Olson. Emeka is a barrister from Nigeria, but he was also head of intercession for the International Christian Chamber of Commerce. Over the many years I knew him, he shared the most amazing stories of miracles in the marketplace.

Several years ago, I hosted a conference and invited him to speak at my event. I asked him to share an experience where God answered prayer in a very direct way that impacted his job as a barrister (attorney). He shared a powerful testimony of the Holy Spirit's guidance in a critical legal case. This story demonstrates how obedience to God's voice can lead to miraculous outcomes.

A Divine Intervention in Court

"When you qualify in Nigeria as a barrister, you are addressed as a solicitor and advocate of the Supreme Court of Nigeria," Emeka began. "I had to handle a case on appeal, and in preparing for it, I wrote a brief outlining five grounds of appeal. My wife, my junior colleague, and I prayed earnestly that morning for divine guidance."

Upon arriving at the court, Emeka sought advice from senior lawyers about the legislation he was dealing with, which was relatively new and lacked established case law. Despite his efforts, he received little help. Feeling the weight of the case, he bowed his head in prayer, seeking the Holy Spirit's direction.

"The Spirit of God told me to cancel grounds 1 to 4 and argue only ground 5," he recounted. When it was his turn to speak, he informed the judge of his decision.

"Your lordship, I wish to withdraw grounds 1 to 4 and proceed only with ground 5," Emeka said. The judge, surprised by this unusual move, asked, "Counsel, are you sure that's what you want to do?"

"Yes, your lordship," Emeka affirmed.

The judge struck out the first four grounds, and Emeka proceeded with his argument on ground 5. When he finished, the opposing lawyer stood up but was unable to speak. For 12 minutes, he stammered and turned in various directions, finally admitting, "It is unfortunate, my lord, that my learned friend has withdrawn motions 1 to 4. I wish to yield the case."

Later, Emeka discovered that the opposing lawyer had prepared only for grounds 1 to 4 and had no argument for ground 5. Emeka's obedience to the Holy Spirit had won the case.

Summary:

- **Promise:** *"My sheep hear My voice, and I know them, and they follow Me." -John 10:27*

- **Problem:** Emeka needed to argue five points before the Supreme Court. God instructed him to focus only on point 5.

- **Miracle:** The opposing lawyer was unprepared for point 5 and yielded the case, leading to Emeka's victory.

Jesus, Savior of the World, Sentenced to Death

During the Biden administration in America, we saw the weaponization of the legal system against conservatives and especially Donald Trump. Truth was being manipulated to defeat the enemies of the left.

Jesus experienced this same weaponization against him through the Pharisees. The legal system was not kind to Jesus. It led to His crucifixion. His crucifixion is the cornerstone of our Christian faith, representing the ultimate sacrifice for humanity's sins. The scriptures tell us He was arrested, tried by the Sanhedrin, and sentenced by Pontius Pilate to be scourged and crucified. His death became the salvation for all mankind.

The disciples were thrown into chaos, not knowing what was happening. Peter denied Jesus three times. Their world was falling apart. The three years they had just experienced seemed like a dream that was being destroyed. The disciples fled until Jesus appeared to them after the crucifixion.

Jesus was stripped of His clothing and offered vinegar mixed with myrrh or gall to drink after He declared, "I am thirsty." He was then crucified at Golgotha between two thieves. According to the Gospel of Mark, He was nailed to the cross at the third hour (9 a.m.) and died at the ninth hour (3 p.m.).

Above His cross, a sign declared, "Jesus of Nazareth, King of the Jews," written in Hebrew, Latin, and Greek. Soldiers divided His garments and cast lots for His seamless robe. After His death, a soldier pierced His side with a spear, causing blood and water to flow out, fulfilling prophecy.

The Bible records seven statements Jesus made from the cross and describes supernatural events surrounding His death. Collectively referred to as the Passion, Jesus' suffering and death are central to the Gospel, symbolizing salvation and atonement.

Summary:

Promise: *"For God so loved the world that He gave His only begotten Son, that whoever believes in Him should not perish but have everlasting life" - John 3:16*

Problem: Jesus was wrongfully accused and conspired against by the Jewish leaders, who persuaded Pontius Pilate to crucify Him. His disciples thought he came to free the Jewish people from the oppression of the Romans. Jesus asked the Father to forgive them, for they knew not what they were doing.

Miracle: Jesus died but rose from the dead, giving eternal life to all who believe in Him. *"For Christ also suffered once for sins, the righteous for the unrighteous, to bring you to God" - 1 Peter 3:18*

Chapter 7– "I need you to speak, Lord!" - The 40 Day Fast

From 1994 to 2001, I endured a major season of adversity in my life. I faced many losses and sought God to understand what He was doing in my life. Despite my prayers, I wasn't receiving the clarity I needed. Determined to hear from God, I resolved to fast until I received an answer.

Initially, I thought the fast might last two or three days, but after three days, I still hadn't discerned anything. I pressed on for another three days—still nothing. Each day brought the same silence, yet I continued, holding onto faith. By the thirtieth day, I still hadn't heard anything. Finally, on the fortieth day of fasting, I attended a conference in Mississippi.

During the conference, a young man with a distinct South African accent took the podium. He shared a prophetic message for someone in the audience who had been enduring great adversity for several years. Using verses from Hosea, his words echoed scriptures God had repeatedly spoken to me from Hosea, an unusual book to get direction.

The detailed description of my struggles left no doubt—God was speaking to me through this man. His name was Bradley Stuart. Bradley, who had a ministry of intercession, and had been experiencing gradual healing from cerebral palsy over the last several years.

The next day, I met with Bradley for prayer. I had been wrestling with whether to restart a magazine that had failed due to insufficient capital. I'd already lost $50,000 on the magazine. During our prayer time, Bradley shared these words: "I don't believe God is raising up the magazine. But He is raising up something that seems insignificant in your eyes."

At the time, I couldn't fathom what that might be. Later, I realized he was referring to the devotional I had started writing called *TGIF: Today God Is First.* Little did I know, *TGIF* would become the cornerstone of an international ministry God was birthing that would be read in 105 countries and have 200,000 daily subcribers.

Bradley and I became close friends over the years. He joined my intercession team, and we traveled to conferences worldwide. Even today, he continues to be a vital part of our ministry's prayer support.

Summary

Promise: *"However, this kind does not go out except by prayer and fasting." – Matthew 17:21*

Problem: Needed answers and direction from God.

Miracle: God gave direction on the 40th day of a fast.

"Where's Your Angel?"

Bradley shared a powerful story of an angel encounter that took place in 1997.

"I joined a team for an outreach in South Africa, just north of Johannesburg. As we prepared, the Lord impressed upon us to focus our prayers more on the safety of the team than the outreach itself.

Once there, we mobilized and began evangelizing in different communities. Suddenly, we heard a commotion in the distance. A large group of 16,000 rebellious youth was approaching with the intent to attack us. We quickly ran into our tents and began praying fervently. About 45 minutes later, everything grew silent. When we stepped outside, we saw the mob fleeing, and moments later, the army arrived. We praised God for sending the army to rescue us.

Six weeks later, we returned to the same area to evangelize again. Shortly after arriving, one of the youths from the previous encounter approached us.

'Where is your angel?' he demanded. 'Don't hide your angel!'

Perplexed, we asked, 'What are you talking about?'

He explained, 'When we came to attack you, your leader raised his hands, and a huge angel appeared behind him. The angel rebuked us in our mother tongue, and we fled. We could have burned everything before the army arrived, but the fear of the Lord came upon us because of that angel.'

Angels Hold Up Our Bus

In 2002, I led a prayer journey around the island of Taiwan. Our team traveled in a double-decker bus, and a group back at a local church in Taiwan interceded for us throughout the journey.

On the third day, as we traveled along a narrow mountain road, the bus tipped onto its side and began sliding down the mountainside. A few small trees miraculously stopped us from plunging hundreds of feet into the valley below. Astonishingly, everyone emerged unharmed.

Later, the intercession team in Taiwan shared a vision they had during that exact moment. They saw angels holding the bus to prevent it from falling. We knew then it wasn't the trees that saved us—it was God's angels at work, miraculously preserving our lives."

Summary

Promise: *"He who dwells in the secret place of the Most High*
shall abide under the shadow of the Almighty.
I will say of the LORD, 'He is my refuge and my fortress;
My God, in Him I will trust.'"

Surely He shall deliver you from the snare of the [a] *fowler*
And from the perilous pestilence.
He shall cover you with His feathers,
And under His wings you shall take refuge;
His truth shall be your shield and buckler.
You shall not be afraid of the terror by night,
Nor of the arrow that flies by day,
Nor of the pestilence that walks in darkness,
Nor of the destruction that lays waste at noonday.

A thousand may fall at your side,
And ten thousand at your right hand;
But it shall not come near you.
Only with your eyes shall you look,
And see the reward of the wicked.

Because you have made the LORD, who is my refuge,
Even the Most High, your dwelling place,
No evil shall befall you,
Nor shall any plague come near your dwelling;

For He shall give His angels charge over you,
To keep you in all your ways. – Psalm 91:1-11

Problem: Rebellious youth were attacking the ministry team.
Risk of bus going off the road and cliff.

Miracle: God sent His angels to save them on both occasions.

A Biblical Reminder of Angelic Intervention

These stories remind me of Acts 12, where Peter's miraculous escape from prison showcases the power of God and the ministry of angels:

"Now behold, an angel of the Lord stood by him, and a light shone in the prison; and he struck Peter on the side and raised him up, saying, 'Arise quickly!' And his chains fell off his hands. Then the angel said to him, 'Gird yourself and tie on your sandals…'" - Acts 12:7-8

Like Peter, God's intervention in our lives often comes through His angels, who guard, guide, and deliver us. Bradley's stories serve as a powerful testament to the reality of angelic protection and the sovereign hand of God at work in our lives. God also honored my 40-day fast by answering my prayer on the last day.

Chapter 8 - The Power of Prophetic Encounters

I was raised in a conservative home. We attended church every Sunday. I was baptized when I was 12-years old. But like many young people, it didn't stick. I would not fully embrace Christ until I was 22 years old. Strangely, the man who was instrumental in my conversion was a southern Baptist pastor who had been an assistant pastor at the church where I grew up.

I had moved to North Myrtle Beach to get away from my mother after college because she was preaching to me about Christ but I wasn't ready. However, within 2 years I was ripe for the Gospel because of my failure to achieve my goal of playing professional golf. I began searching for answers to life's greatest questions about my life purpose. And God provided Pastor Jim to give me the answers.

In 1994 my world fell apart. I had major financial losses from my business and my wife filed for divorce. My daughter was nearing 18 now and I had been paying child support and alimony until she reached 18. Once she reached 18 my commitment was fulfilled, and it created some uncertainty about her future living situation. I went out to dinner with my daughter and saw the emotional pain she was in and how concerned she was. I was broken over what the devil had done in my marriage and family. I was also trying to work on myself to take responsibility for my part in allowing it to happen. But there were some things that simply could not be fixed no matter what I did.

That night I had a meltdown. I began to weep over what I saw that night in my daughter. I was angry at the devil for destroying my family. "Why is this happening God!?" I was broken and barely getting by. I had gotten down to my last $1000 but by God's grace I was able to keep the property I was living in that also served as my office.

That property was a house on 4 acres that I purchased years earlier from the popular Christian singer, Don Francisco. Don was known for a hit song, "He's Alive" that won a Dove Award and Dolly Parton made it famous when she recorded it. Don was part of a home group that was connected to Calvary Chapel Atlanta where I had worked for 3 months when I first came to Atlanta.

Don had his own challenges in life at that time as his wife was an alcoholic and he struggled with how to handle it. Don decided to move out west and when I learned about this, I asked him if he was going to sell his house. He said, "Yes" and I asked how much he wanted. Money was tight for me, so I was not able to come up with a down payment. Don sacrificed what he could have made on the house and creatively made a way for me to buy his house at an extremely below market price. That was a huge blessing at a time when I didn't have too many positive things going on in my life. During the divorce settlement my wife would get the 13-acre horse property we had recently purchased, and I would get this property. Little would I know how valuable this property would become many years later.

The Prophet

I mentioned that I came from a very conservative church background. However, God was exposing me to men and women who had unique spiritual gifts such as words of knowledge and prophecy, something that was brand new to me.

I was invited to speak at a marketplace conference in Minneapolis. I had gotten to know a business guy who owned a dental company. He was a prayer warrior, and he was praying for people in the basement of the church. He came to me during the conference and said, "We are praying for people in the basement and want to pray for you. God is in the basement!"

"Well, if God is in the basement I must surely come down!"

I walked into the room and my friend was there with another man I never met. They asked me to sit down, and they were going to "pray" for me. It was no kind of prayer I had ever experienced. The man began to prophesy to me.

"The Lord shows me you have a daughter who has great gifts in poetry. She has been in a stronghold for several years. The Lord says God is turning the daughter's heart to the father's heart and she will be coming home." I was amazed at the words he was speaking. The idea she would come to live with me was way out there. She was in no emotional state to meet with me. She had been into New Age, rebellious, and was not in a good place.

He continued speaking other words to me that were encouraging and very detailed for someone who had never met me. Finally, when I stood up and approached the door he said, "And, oh, by the way, the Lord wants you to know He has seen the tears you shed for your daughter in your bedroom."

That broke the floodgate! I began to weep. How can he know that? I knew God knew me at that point in my life. He knew everything I was going through. He really was working on my behalf. For the first time I sensed my Father loved me.

I would continue to experience these divine encounters. My new prophetic friend would become a good friend to our family, and we would begin to travel together. We began to minister together. I would teach and he would minister prophetically to those was handpicked. I realized my friend and I were walking out Ephesians 2:20: *"Now, therefore, you are no longer strangers and foreigners, but fellow citizens with the saints and members of the household of God, having been built on the foundation of the apostles and prophets, Jesus Christ Himself being the chief cornerstone..." Ephesians 2:19-20*

God showed me I was an apostolic teacher to the marketplace and my friend was God's prophetic voice to break through difficult strongholds in the lives of leaders.

"Whenever I see you, I see the word 'WRITE' on your forehead."

During this season of my life many people knew the challenges I had been facing. I got to know Dr. C. Peter Wagner, a theologian and former seminary professor, in the mid-nineties when God began to use me and other leaders to birth the faith@work movement. I was in the first four years of my adversity when I was attending a meeting at the International Prayer Center in Colorado Springs by invitation of Peter Wagner. One of the attendees was Cindy Jacobs. Cindy was a recognized prophetess in the nation. We had met but didn't really know each other well. I was walking down the aisle when Cindy approached me and said, "Os, I don't know what God is doing with you but every time I see you, I see the word 'WRITE' on your forehead. You are going to write many books!"

I'd never written a book. I was a C- student in school. I knew nothing about writing books. However, over the next several years God would prompt me to begin reflecting what I was learning and seeing take place. My first writing began with a devotional series sharing what I was learning about my adversity and what God said about work and calling. I first began sharing these simple messages with friends on my email list. Then, a friend who had a website that later became Crosswalk.com came to me and said, "Os, these messages are powerful. You need to share them with a larger audience. Let me put these on my website and I will send them out for you."

When he began to do that, I began to get letters from all over the world. They all said the same thing: "You read my mail today. You are describing exactly what I am going through." These devotionals later became a book in 2000 and then shortly after that the buyer of the Family Christian Bookstores reached out to me and said he was an avid fan of my devotional that was now called TGIF Today God Is First. He asked me if I would write three 100-page books for their stores on the topic of money, work and hearing God.

That would be the beginning of a writing career that would allow me to write more than two dozen books and take me to 26 countries to train leaders as of this writing.

"You're Considering Suicide!"

God began to open doors for me to speak at conferences and churches around the country and even in other countries. I often took my prophetic friend with me to minister. I had a trip planned for Los Angeles when someone on my TGIF list heard of my visit. He asked if he could pick me up from the airport and take me to meet a Christian filmmaker who owned a large 5-city block studio space.

I met this man and ministered to him. He was impacted by what I shared with him and offered to host my half-day Change Agent workshop. It was a powerful meeting of Hollywood leaders. The afternoon before our meeting we hosted a gathering of about 15 Christian leaders working in Hollywood. I had my prophetic friend with me for these meetings. One of the women I met was Karen Covell who was the founder of the Hollywood Prayer Network. I told her I wanted my friend to pray for her. She agreed.

About 30 minutes later Karen runs towards me with tears in her eyes and said, "That man told me things no one on this earth knows about me! I never knew there were people on earth like this! I want every person I know in Hollywood to have the same experience I just had!"

That began a five-year season of three to four one week trips a year to Hollywood to minister to people Karen would invite to her office for ministry from me and my friend. She would bring them into her office for 20-minute appointments with us.

One man came into our meeting room. He had a solemn look on his face. The minute he sat down my prophetic friend says, "I see what you are about to do. I see the gun. I see what has happened with you and your wife and your business."

Wow! I was blown away with the words that my friend was speaking. I concluded that either these were true or this was going to be our last visit to Hollywood. He was really out on a limb with this one!

We concluded the session and the man walked out of the room with no indication that what we said was true or not. However, once we broke for lunch Karen came rushing into the room.

"Oh my gosh! You are not going to believe what happened! You just saved that man's life! He was about to commit suicide."

The man's business was in crisis and his wife was leaving him. He had no hope and was ready to end his life.

The man turned out to be a Hollywood producer who made the film, Pursuit of Happiness, with Will Smith as the lead actor. It was a story about a man in deep crisis and homeless. He was literally living the story of his movie.

We became friends over the next few years, and I helped him navigate his season of adversity. It took several months, but he is now in a good place in his life.

Summary

Promise: *"For I know the thoughts that I think toward you, says the* LORD, *thoughts of peace and not of evil, to give you a future and a hope." – Jeremiah 29:11*

Problem: A Hollywood producer had lost hope in his life circumstances.

Miracle: God used the prophetic gift of my friend to reveal God's love for the producer and save his life.

"Don't go to Jerusalem!" - Agabus and Paul

In the book of Acts, we encounter a remarkable story that highlights the delicate balance between prophetic revelation and human responsibility. This story unfolds in Acts 21:10-14, where a prophet named Agabus delivers a dire warning to the apostle Paul. Though the prophecy was accurate, Paul's response reveals an essential truth—prophetic words are not mandates, but invitations to discernment.

This chapter explores the context of Agabus' prophecy, Paul's decision to move forward despite the warning, and the critical application of understanding that while prophets may reveal God's will, the actions that follow remain in the hands of the recipient. This principle has profound implications for how we respond to prophetic words in our own lives.

The Prophecy of Agabus

After Paul had completed his third missionary journey, he traveled toward Jerusalem with a deep sense of calling and purpose. In Acts 20:22-23, Paul acknowledged that the Holy Spirit had already testified to him in every city that "chains and tribulations" awaited him. Despite this forewarning, Paul was resolute in his commitment to go to Jerusalem, saying, *"I am ready not only to be bound, but also to die at Jerusalem for the name of the Lord Jesus."* -Acts 21:13

When Paul and his companions arrived in Caesarea, they stayed at the house of Philip the evangelist. It was here that Agabus, a seasoned prophet, came down from Judea with a vivid prophetic act.

"Coming over to us, he took Paul's belt, tied his own hands and feet with it and said, 'The Holy Spirit says, "In this way the Jewish leaders in Jerusalem will bind the owner of this belt and will hand him over to the Gentiles."'" - Acts 21:11, NIV

Agabus' prophecy was both clear and symbolic. By taking Paul's belt and binding his hands and feet, he graphically illustrated the fate that awaited Paul in Jerusalem. The prophecy was a stark warning, and its fulfillment was undeniable. Paul was indeed arrested, bound, and handed over to the Romans shortly after arriving in Jerusalem.

Paul's Response: Prophetic Revelation Versus Apostolic Resolve

The reaction to Agabus' prophecy was swift and emotional. Those who heard the word—both Paul's companions and the local believers—pleaded with Paul not to go to Jerusalem. They interpreted the prophecy as a divine warning, urging Paul to avoid the impending danger.

But Paul's response was unwavering:

"Why are you weeping and breaking my heart? I am ready not only to be bound, but also to die in Jerusalem for the name of the Lord Jesus." - Acts 21:13, NIV

Paul's decision to proceed to Jerusalem, despite the prophetic warning, offers a profound insight: Prophetic words may reveal what is coming, but they do not always dictate what we must do. Paul understood that Agabus had spoken the truth—he would face persecution—but Paul's calling compelled him to move forward regardless of the consequences.

Understanding Prophetic Warnings: Revelation Versus Application

The story of Paul and Agabus highlights an essential principle in responding to prophetic words: Prophecy provides revelation, but the application is determined by the one who receives it.

1. **Prophecy Reveals, But Does Not Command**

   Prophetic words, even when accurate, are not always directives. Agabus revealed what would happen, but he did not tell Paul what he *must* do in response. Paul had to weigh the prophetic word against the inner witness of the Holy Spirit and his own sense of divine assignment. Requiring someone to follow the action of a prophetic word moves us into witchcraft, which the scripture prohibits.

This principle reminds us that God often reveals possibilities, not inevitabilities. Prophetic words can be warnings, confirmations, or encouragements, but they rarely replace the need for prayer, discernment, and Spirit-led decision-making by the one receiving the word.

2. **Prophetic Words Invite Discernment**

   Paul's decision to move forward despite the warning was not a rejection of Agabus' prophecy but rather an acknowledgment that God's purposes sometimes require walking through hardship. Paul discerned that the prophecy was not a prohibition, but a preparation.

   In our own lives, when we receive a prophetic word—whether a warning, an encouragement, or a promise—it is our responsibility to take that word before the Lord, seeking His wisdom and guidance. As 1 Thessalonians 5:20-21 exhorts us: *"Do not despise prophecies. Test all things; hold fast what is good."*

3. **Prophetic Warnings Can Prepare, Not Prevent**

   Paul was not oblivious to the dangers that awaited him. Agabus' prophecy was not a deterrent but a divine preparation. Paul knew what was coming, and that knowledge fortified his resolve. Sometimes, God allows us to see the challenges ahead not so that we avoid them, but so that we face them with courage and faith.

   Consider Jesus' words to His disciples: *"In this world you will have trouble. But take heart! I have overcome the world." - John 16:33* Prophetic warnings may reveal trouble ahead, but they also invite us to lean into God's grace and strength.

Application: How to Respond to Prophetic Words Today

The example of Paul and Agabus serves as a guide for how we can respond to prophetic words in our own journey of faith. Here are three key principles to apply:

1. Weigh Every Word with the Holy Spirit

No matter how accurate or dramatic a prophetic word may be, we are called to bring it before God. Prophetic words are not substitutes for a personal relationship with the Lord. As Jesus said in John 10:27, *"My sheep listen to my voice; I know them, and they follow me."* Discernment comes through intimacy with God.

2. Distinguish Between Warning and Prohibition

Just because a prophetic word highlights potential danger does not mean God is saying to avoid it. Sometimes, warnings prepare us to endure, not escape. When facing a prophetic word of caution, ask: "Is this a warning to change course or a preparation for what's ahead?"

3. Act in Alignment with Your Calling

Paul was willing to walk into danger because he was convinced of his calling. Prophetic words must be weighed against God's assignment for your life. If the prophetic word aligns with your purpose but suggests hardship, ask for strength rather than an exit.

Final Thoughts: Prophecy and Personal Responsibility

Agabus was right—Paul was bound and delivered to the Gentiles. But Paul was also right—his journey to Jerusalem led to the furtherance of the gospel and the fulfillment of God's plan. This story reminds us that prophecy invites us to engage with God's plan, but it does not remove the need for personal obedience and discernment.

When we receive a prophetic word, may we, like Paul, seek the heart of God and move forward with boldness, knowing that sometimes, the path of obedience leads through difficulty. Yet, in those moments, we can be confident that God's grace will sustain us, and His purposes will be fulfilled.

As we navigate the prophetic in our lives, let us hold fast to this truth: Prophecy informs, but obedience transforms.

Summary

Promise: *"But the manifestation of the Spirit is given to each one for the profit of all: for to one is given the word of wisdom through the Spirit, to another the word of knowledge through the same Spirit, to another faith by the same Spirit, to another gifts of healings by the same Spirit, [1]to another the working of miracles, to another prophecy, to another discerning of spirits, to another different kinds of tongues, to another the interpretation of tongues. But one and the same Spirit works all these things, distributing to each one individually as He wills." - 1 Corinthians 12:7-11*

Problem: I was discouraged and needed hope in my life. The Hollywood producer had lost all hope. Paul was warned about upcoming persecution in Jerusalem.

Miracle: God used a prophet to give a word of prophecy to me and my Hollywood friend to help us break through our discouragement and give new hope. God used Agabus to warn Paul about upcoming persecution in Jerusalem, but wrongly tried to convince him not to go.

Chapter 9 - "Speak to Your Mountain!"

Does God do miracles in business? Is He concerned about the mountains we face in our life? Does He want us to bring the everyday problems we face in the workplace to His attention? The answer to every one of these questions is yes. God wants to be involved in every aspect of our lives. God exhorts us to use our faith to move the mountains in our lives.

Jesus replied, "Let the faith of God be in you. Listen to the truth I speak to you: If someone says to this mountain with great faith and having no doubt, 'Mountain, be lifted up and thrown into the midst of the sea, and believes that what he says will happen, it will be done. - Mark 11:22,23

Gunnar Olson, the Swedish founder of the International Christian Chamber of Commerce, tells a story about God performing a miracle in his own business several years ago. He was founder of a plastics company in Sweden. They made huge plastic bags that were used to cover bales of hay in the farmlands across Europe. It was the harvest season and they were getting ready to ship thousands of pallets of these bags to their customers. More than 1,000 pallets were ready to ship when an alarming discovery was made. Every bag on the warehouse floor had sealed shut from top to bottom. Scientists declared the entire stock as worthless trash. Nothing could be done. The company would go out of business.

Gunnar, his wife, and children sought the Lord in prayer about this catastrophe. The Holy Spirit spoke through various family members. The wife said, "If God can turn water into wine, what are plastics?" The daughter said, "I don't believe this is from the Lord. We should stand against it."

Gunnar sensed they were to trust God for a miracle in this situation. They began to pray. They took authority over this mountain of a problem based on Mark 11, which gave them the authority to cast a mountain into the sea if faith only the size of a mustard seed could be exercised.

On Sunday night Gunnar stood outside his plant and said, "Listen heaven, listen earth, who is the Lord over Alphapac? It's Jesus. I now command all the bags to rotate back to their original place!" He and his family went inside the warehouse and laid hands on every pallet, asking the Lord to restore the bags to their original condition. It took several hours.

On Monday the employees began to inspect the bags again. As they inspected the bags, they discovered that every single bag had been restored to its original condition! An incredible miracle had taken place. The inspectors who inspected the original problem returned to validate that a miracle had taken place.

Summary

Promise: God owned Gunnar's business. God is his provider.

Problem: Crisis in manufacturing that could put him out of business.

Miracle: Gunnar used his authority to speak to him mountain and God restored bags.

Moses: The Rock and the Breakthrough

Moses stood at the helm of one of history's greatest deliverances. Chosen by God to lead the Israelites out of slavery in Egypt, he bore the weight of a monumental promise: to bring God's people into the Promised Land. It was a promise steeped in hope, yet fraught with challenges that tested Moses' resolve, faith, and obedience.

One such challenge arose in the wilderness of Zin. The Israelites, weary and parched, began to grumble against Moses and Aaron. Their cries echoed a familiar refrain: "Why did you bring us out of Egypt to this barren place? We and our livestock will die of thirst!" The problem was immediate and pressing—there was no water.

Faced with the clamor of a desperate people, Moses turned to God. The Lord gave a clear and extraordinary instruction: *"Speak to that rock before their eyes and it will pour out its water" - Numbers 20:7* Here was a moment for divine intervention, an opportunity for God to demonstrate His power and faithfulness through Moses.

Even so, the miracle underscores a powerful principle: God's faithfulness is not dependent on our perfection. Despite Moses' misstep, God provided for His people. The rock, struck or spoken to, became a vessel of supernatural breakthrough.

The Spiritual Lesson: Authority for Breakthrough

This story reveals the authority believers have to decree God's promises into reality. The instruction to speak to the rock underscores the power of declaration. Job 22:28 affirms this truth: *"You will also declare a thing, and it will be established for you; so light will shine on your ways."*

When natural solutions are exhausted, God invites us to operate in the authority He has given us. Speaking His Word over situations—making decrees aligned with His promises—can unlock breakthroughs where human effort falls short.

Activate the Promise

In your own life, identify the "rock" you are facing. What situation seems immovable, impossible, or barren? Instead of striving in your own strength, turn to God's Word and make a decree of faith:

- Declare provision where there is lack.
- Declare healing where there is sickness.
- Declare peace where there is turmoil.

The same God who provided water in the wilderness will meet your needs. His promises are steadfast, and His power knows no bounds.

As you align your words with His promises, you activate heaven's resources to bring forth miracles in your life. The authority to speak to your "rock" lies in your faith and obedience. Remember, the breakthrough is not about what you can do but about trusting the One who can do all things.

In the end, Moses' story reminds us that even when we falter, God's grace abounds. His purposes will prevail, and His promises will come to pass. Take heart and speak to your rock—your miracle awaits.

Summary

Promise: God will take Israelites into the Promised Land and provide for them.

Problem: They were in desparate need of water.

Miracle: Moses struck the rock for water but instead of speaking to the rock, Moses stuck the rock and would not be able to enter the Promised Land because of his disobedience.

Chapter 10 - Redeeming the Queen

Pam once reigned as "Queen Pam," a Madam who built an empire trading in drugs and sex. In the shadows of her big city operation, she lived in a luxurious home with a Hummer in the driveway, surrounded by wealth and power. Yet beneath the glittering facade was a woman whose soul was held hostage by shame, addiction, and pain—a woman desperately searching for a way out.

Pam's descent into darkness began in her early years, growing up in a small Georgia town with a family fractured by dysfunction. Her biological father was an abusive alcoholic, and her mother, a free-spirited former Playboy Bunny, offered little stability. At just five years old, Pam's innocence was stolen when her father promised her the stray puppy she'd found in the yard—if she would come upstairs. Instead of receiving love, she endured betrayal and abuse, a wound that shaped her understanding of love and self-worth.

"That day, I learned that I could get what I wanted by going upstairs," Pam recalled.

When Pam told her mother, her father was kicked out, but the damage had been done. Worse still, the abuse continued at the hands of other family members. By the time she was nine, Pam had discovered marijuana lying around the house, using it to escape the pain. "When I smoked pot, I felt free," she said. But drugs were only the beginning.

In her teens, Pam turned to harder substances like cocaine and found fleeting solace in sex. With every encounter, she sought love and validation, but she was left only with deeper wounds. By her twenties, Pam had been married three times, each relationship reinforcing her belief that she was nothing more than an object.

"I was a whore. I was filth. That's all I knew about myself," Pam admitted.

But amidst the chaos, a seed of hope had been planted. A country preacher who was a guest at her godly grandmothers for Sunday lunch had once prophesied over her life: "This one is special. She's going to do great things for God one day." That voice echoed in Pam's heart, even as she spiraled further into despair.

By her mid-twenties, Pam's life reached a breaking point. Addicted to drugs and consumed by shame, she prepared to inject a lethal dose of cocaine. In desperation, she cried out, "God, if You're real, help me. Rescue me."

At that moment, she heard the voice again: "You don't belong here. You're going to do great things for God."

With renewed strength, Pam abandoned the syringe and checked into rehab. She began attending church and committed to following Christ. For two years, she stayed clean and refrained from sex. But one moment of weakness sent her spiraling back into her old life. The shame of her failure convinced her she was unworthy of God's love.

This cycle of shame and addiction trapped Pam for the next 25 years. Living just outside Atlanta, she became a successful drug dealer and Madam, convincing herself that she was helping other women escape worse situations.

"I thought I was doing them a favor," Pam said. "But deep down, I knew I was selling my soul to the devil."

In 2010, Pam's double life caught up with her. Arrested for drug possession, she was sentenced to five years in prison. In her cell, she requested a Bible. As she read, she felt God's love flooding her heart, breaking through the chains of guilt and self-loathing.

"I had to repent of everything—prostitution, using my body, putting drugs into it," Pam said. "God filled me with His love, a liquid love I can't describe."

For the first time, Pam forgave her abusers and released them to God. "He not only healed my heart but theirs too," she said, adding that many of them came to Christ through her prayers.

While in prison, Pam started a scripture-reading ministry, sharing the transformative power of Jesus with other inmates. She changed her name to Pamela, signifying her new life. After serving only 18 months, she was released in 2011.

"My purpose now is to help the disenfranchised, the less fortunate, and those forgotten behind prison walls," she said.

Today, Pamela runs LifeChangers Legacy**,** a ministry that mentors hundreds of men and women using her curriculum, *I See Me Free.*

Pamela's journey is a testament to God's redeeming love. "It doesn't matter what you've been through. There is a way out, and His name is Jesus," she said. "Allow Him to guide you into the purpose He has for your life."

Pamela's story reminds us that even the most broken lives can be restored. God's love is greater than shame, and His grace reaches into the darkest places to bring healing and hope.

I met Pamela in 2015 at a movie premier, strangely about a drug addict woman that one of my board members asked me to speak at that he was the producer. I had been single for 7 years. She had been single for 15 years. Our meeting led to other meetings, and we began dating. We were married nine months later. And today we are happily married. She has been a blessing in my life and has overcome great odds to become a godly woman that God is using in amazing ways.

Promise: "She's going to do great things for God one day." – pastor

> *"For I know the thoughts that I think toward you, says the LORD, thoughts of peace and not of evil, to give you a future and a hope." – Jeremiah 29:11*

Problem: Sexually abused from age 5. Satan wanted to steal, kill and destroy her life. (John 10:10)

Miracle: Pam was arrested and sent to prison for 18 months. Prison became her place of freedom. God rescued Pam in prison where she birthed LifeChangers Legacy prison ministry, a curriculum that helps others gain freedom from destructive life patterns. Pamela's new spiritual name is Pamela, recognizing her new life in Christ. www.LifeChangersLegacy.org

Mary Magdalene - A Witness to Transformation and Resurrection

Mary Magdalene is a prominent figure in the New Testament, mentioned in all four Gospels. Her life and role in Jesus' ministry and resurrection provide rich insights into her significance in the early Christian faith. She is an enduring symbol of transformation, devotion, and courage, offering lessons for all believers.

Mary Magdalene's name reveals her origins: she was from Magdala, a town on the western shore of the Sea of Galilee. The Gospels portray her as a devoted follower of Jesus who played a critical role in His ministry, crucifixion, and resurrection. Her life is a testament to the transformative power of encountering Jesus and the depth of her commitment to Him.

One of the earliest mentions of Mary Magdalene highlights her deliverance from seven demons. Both Luke 8:2 and Mark 16:9 describe this event, indicating a profound spiritual transformation. Though the exact nature of her affliction is not detailed, the fact that Jesus cast out seven demons underscores the depth of His healing power. This act of deliverance set Mary on a path of unwavering devotion to her Savior.

Mary Magdalene's faithfulness is evident in her active role in Jesus' ministry. She is mentioned among a group of women who supported Jesus and His disciples financially (Luke 8:1–3). Her contributions, along with those of other women, provided the resources necessary for the spread of the Gospel. Mary's actions reflect her deep gratitude and loyalty to Jesus, whom she followed closely throughout His ministry.

Mary Magdalene's devotion to Jesus remained steadfast, even during His crucifixion. While many of His followers fled in fear, she was among the few who stayed (Matthew 27:55–56, Mark 15:40, John 19:25). Her courage and presence at the foot of the cross demonstrate her unwavering commitment to Jesus, even in the face of danger and immense sorrow.

After Jesus' death, Mary Magdalene followed His body to the tomb, observing as Joseph of Arimathea laid Him to rest (Matthew 27:61, Mark 15:47). Her attention to these details shows her deep desire to honor Him, even in death. She was determined to ensure that His body was treated with the utmost care and respect.

Mary Magdalene's most significant role came on the morning of Jesus' resurrection.

• At the Tomb: Early on the first day of the week, Mary went to the tomb to anoint Jesus' body (Matthew 28:1, Mark 16:1–2, John 20:1). To her astonishment, she found the tomb empty.

• Encounter with Angels: Along with other women, Mary encountered angels who announced that Jesus had risen (Matthew 28:5–7, Mark 16:5–7, Luke 24:4–7). This moment marked the beginning of the resurrection proclamation.

• Encounter with the Risen Christ: In John 20:11–18, Mary Magdalene became the first person to see the risen Jesus. Mistaking Him for the gardener, she recognized Him when He called her by name. Jesus then commissioned her to share the news with His disciples, making her the first to proclaim the resurrection. For this reason, she is often called the "apostle to the apostles."

Mary Magdalene's story has often been clouded by misconceptions:

• Not a Prostitute: Despite widespread belief, there is no biblical evidence that Mary Magdalene was a repentant prostitute. This misidentification likely arose from conflating her with other unnamed women in the Gospels.

• Later Traditions: Over the centuries, Mary Magdalene became a symbol of repentance and devotion in Christian tradition. However, the biblical narrative emphasizes her role as a faithful disciple and witness to the resurrection rather than focusing on any sinful past.

Mary Magdalene's role as the first witness to the risen Christ highlights the equality and dignity Jesus extended to women. In a time when women's testimonies were often disregarded, Jesus entrusted her with the most important message of all: the proclamation of His resurrection. Her story underscores the centrality of women in spreading the Gospel and the transformative power of encountering Jesus.

Mary Magdalene remains a powerful example of transformation, devotion, and courage in the Christian faith.

Her journey from deliverance to becoming the first witness of the resurrection illustrates the profound impact of encountering Jesus. As a faithful follower and the bearer of the resurrection message, her life continues to inspire believers to this day.

Summary

Promise: *"For God so loved the world that He gave His only begotten son that whosoever believes in Him shall have eternal life." – John 3:16*

Problem: She was demon possessed.

Miracle: Jesus cast out the demons. She became an avid supporter of Jesus and traveled with Jesus and the disciples.

Chapter 11 - "This Is My House!"

In the previous chapter I shared about my meeting Pamela at a movie preview of *Captive*, a film based on a true story. It recounted the harrowing experience of Ashley Smith, a drug-addicted woman who was taken hostage by Brian Nichols—a man who had killed two people in Atlanta before fleeing to the suburbs. He abducted Ashley in her apartment parking lot at 2 a.m. while she was retrieving cigarettes from her car. The next eight hours would determine whether she would become his next victim.

Ashley was a recovering drug addict. Her life took an unexpected turn during the ordeal. Her mother had given her a copy of *The Purpose Driven Life*, which was sitting on her coffee table. Nichols, in a surprising moment, asked her to read from it. Ashley later credited that book with saving her life.

I had been invited to speak at the film's preview in downtown Atlanta by a board member of my organization, who happened to be the film's Hollywood-based director. As I entered the theater, I recognized a former advertising client who introduced me to Pamela. She mentioned that she had recently received a movie contract and was eager to get my input.

Curious, I asked her, "What about your life has inspired a movie?"

Her reply was cryptic yet intriguing: "It's complicated."

That answer piqued my interest, so I invited her to lunch to learn more. We met the following week, and the conversation quickly revealed a connection. I had been single for seven years; Pamela, for fifteen. What began as a casual meeting developed rapidly, and within nine months, we were married.

Claiming the Promise

During our engagement, Pamela faced a challenge. She needed to move out of her mountain home, but there was a problem: she had five dogs. Finding a rental property that would accommodate them was almost impossible.

After a long search, we finally found a house that seemed perfect. Even more surprising, the landlord was willing to accept the dogs. Excited, we contacted the real estate agent to put down a deposit.

A few hours later, the agent called back with bad news. "I'm sorry, but the house is under contract with an Apple executive. His credit checks out, and unless something changes, the house is his."

Disappointed, I reluctantly called Pamela to share the news. "I hate to tell you this," I began, "but the house isn't available. Someone else has already claimed it."

Her response shocked me. "That's my house! We're still going to the house to pray over it. We'll cancel that contract in the Spirit."

"Pamela, did you hear me? There's already another contract."

"I don't care what they said," she replied firmly. "Meet me there at 2 p.m."

I sighed, but agreed.

At the house, we walked around its perimeter, praying boldly. Pamela declared, "In the name of Jesus, we claim this house! We cancel the other contract, in Jesus' name!"

Her faith was unshakable, but I struggled to match her confidence. Still, I prayed alongside her, asking God to intervene.

We left and continued our day, not knowing what to expect.

A Miracle Unfolds

Later that afternoon, my phone rang. It was the real estate agent. His tone was filled with disbelief.

"I don't know how to explain this," he said, "but the executive has decided not to take the house. It's yours if you still want it."

I could hardly believe what I was hearing. God had answered our prayers.

Pamela and I rejoiced together, overwhelmed by God's faithfulness. I also had to take a moment to repent for my own lack of faith.

This experience taught me a powerful lesson: when you are led by the Spirit to declare God's promises with unwavering faith, He moves in ways that defy logic. Pamela's boldness to stand on God's Word transformed a seemingly impossible situation into a testimony of His power.

Summary

Promise: "*You will also declare a thing, and it will be established for you; So light will shine on your ways.*" – Job 22:28

"And my God shall supply all your need according to His riches in glory by Christ Jesus." – Philippians 4:19

Problem: Pamela needed a rental house that would accept 5 dogs.

Miracle: A previous contract on the house was cancelled because Pamela and Os prayed it would be cancelled.

God Speaks the World Into Existence

Never underestimate the power of your words. The world was created by God by speaking it into existence. God spoke creation into existence, saying, "Let there be light," and light appeared. Throughout chapter 1 of Genesis, God's spoken word brought order, life, and creation into being.

This was the first recorded act of creation. God's spoken word brought light into existence, dispelling the darkness that covered the earth. It underscores the creative and transformative power of God's word to bring illumination and order.

On another occasion, God said, "Let there be a vault between the waters to separate water from water." By speaking, God established the sky, separating the waters above from the waters below. This act set the foundation for the earth's atmosphere, showing God's ability to structure and organize creation through His words.

God said, "Let the water under the sky be gathered to one place, and let dry ground appear." With a simple command, God brought forth the land and the seas, forming the earth's physical landscape. His words created the environment necessary for life to thrive.

God said, "Let the land produce vegetation: seed-bearing plants and trees on the land that bear fruit with seed in it, according to their various kinds." God's words generated life and set in motion the cycle of growth and reproduction. This act of creation demonstrated His ability to bring life and sustainability through spoken command.

God said, "Let there be lights in the vault of the sky to separate the day from the night, and let them serve as signs to mark sacred times, days, and years." God created the sun, moon, and stars to govern time and seasons. These celestial bodies, vital for life and worship, came into being through His spoken word.

God said, "Let the water teem with living creatures, and let birds fly above the earth across the vault of the sky." This marked the creation of animal life in the sea and sky, showing God's authority to populate the earth with diverse life forms by speaking them into existence.

God said, "Let the land produce living creatures according to their kinds: the livestock, the creatures that move along the ground, and the wild animals, each according to its kind." God brought forth animals that would inhabit the earth, emphasizing the diversity and complexity of His creation, all accomplished through His spoken word.

God said, "Let us make mankind in our image, in our likeness, so that they may rule over the fish in the sea and the birds in the sky, over the livestock and all the wild animals, and over all the creatures that move along the ground." God's words culminated in the creation of humanity, made in His image and entrusted with dominion over creation. This declaration highlights the intentionality and relational nature of God's creative power.

In each instance, God's words did not merely describe reality—they created it. His spoken word held the authority to bring forth life and establish order where there was none.

Every word spoken by God aligned perfectly with His divine will and plan. There was no resistance, no delay; creation responded immediately to His voice.

The creation account reflects the potential power of faith-filled words spoken in alignment with God's will. As beings created in His image, we are called to reflect His authority in our own lives by speaking life and truth even in everyday work life situations.

Summary

Promise: *You will also declare a thing, and it will be established for you; So light will shine on your ways. – Job 22:28*

Problem: The world did not exist until God spoke it into existence.

Miracle: God's Word created the earth and all that was in it.

Chapter 12: Hearing God to Buy a Home

"The greatest joy in my life is sitting quietly and hearing God speak to me through His Word," says Andy Mason. Recently I did a podcast interview with Andy, founder of Heaven in Business, to discuss the importance of hearing the voice of God in our marketplace call.

"Hearing God's voice is not just a mystical experience reserved for spiritual elites. It is a deeply personal, intimate connection available to all believers." Andy Mason's story of moving and purchasing a home demonstrates how God speaks in multifaceted ways—through Scripture, people, circumstances, and even moments of uncertainty.

This chapter unpacks how Andy and his family navigated life-altering decisions, learning to trust God's leading step by step by hearing and obeying the voice of God.

The Move That Changed Everything

Andy and his family had moved to the United States from New Zealand, initially planning to stay temporarily. But God had other plans. From the moment they arrived, they began receiving prophetic words from friends and strangers alike:

- "You're here for an extended period."
- "Your green card process will be easy."
- "God is going to give you land in this country."

These affirmations were encouraging yet perplexing. They already had a house and were content with it. But the messages kept coming. One day, a trusted colleague approached Andy, saying, "The Lord told us to buy you a house." This generous offer, though surprising, opened the door to a new phase of trust.

Testing the Word

As Andy and his wife prayed, they felt God leading them to take a step of faith. They put their house on the market, and it sold within three days. The speed of the sale was a clear confirmation that God was orchestrating their steps.

But things took an unexpected turn. The colleague who had promised to buy them a home called with bad news: the funds were no longer available. Andy was stunned. Why would God lead them this far only to shut the door?

Seeking clarity, Andy spent time in prayer at a local house of worship. As he walked and prayed, he heard an internal voice—strong and unmistakable:

"They are not your source of supply. I am."

Guided by this revelation, Andy and his wife found their dream home: a beautiful property with three acres of land, backing onto 20 miles of running trails. But there was one problem—they didn't have the money to purchase it. The owner offered to rent the house to them on the condition that they pay an $80,000 non-refundable deposit, a staggering sum for their financial situation.

Andy wrestled with the decision. As a business consultant, this went against everything he knew about sound financial planning. Yet, he felt God urging him to trust. He sought the counsel of wise friends and mentors, all of whom affirmed the decision. Bolstered by scripture, prayer, and agreement among trusted advisors, they took the leap.

Provision in the Unexpected

Soon after moving in, a wildfire swept through the area, destroying homes and properties around them. Miraculously, their home was spared. The fire even led to insurance funds that allowed them to renovate the property. Despite this provision, they still faced a significant financial shortfall.

With time running out, Andy sought help from trusted individuals. Though hesitant at first, he wrote to six people, sharing his situation. Five of them offered emotional support but couldn't provide financial assistance. The sixth—a successful businessman—turned out to be God's chosen vessel.

After several conversations, the man said:

"The Lord spoke to me today through Psalm 37. The righteous are generous, and their children will inherit the land. You're meant to have this house, and I'm supposed to help you. I'll lend you the remaining funds interest-free, indefinitely."

Andy was overwhelmed with gratitude. The loan allowed them to finalize the purchase, and years later, when they sold the house, the businessman refused repayment, saying, "Your debt is to the Lord, not to me."

Keys to Hearing God's Voice

Andy's story illustrates three key principles for discerning God's voice:

1. **Does it bring life?** God's words carry hope, encouragement, and purpose. They never condemn or sow hopelessness.

2. **Does it bring peace?** When God speaks, there is an inner assurance, even in difficult circumstances. A lack of peace often signals a need for further clarity.

3. **Is it impossible to ignore?** Sometimes, God's instructions challenge our comfort zones. Like Jeremiah, who declared, "Your word is like a fire in my bones; I cannot hold it in" (Jeremiah 20:9), God's calling can compel us to act despite fear or doubt.

The Role of Wise Counsel

Proverbs 11:14 reminds us, *"In the multitude of counselors, there is safety."* Andy emphasizes the importance of seeking advice from seasoned, spiritually mature individuals. Look for those with:

- **Wrinkles and body scars:** Life experience and resilience.
- **Spiritual maturity:** A track record of hearing and obeying God.
- **Freedom from unresolved wounds:** Counselors should offer wisdom without personal biases clouding their perspective.

The Joy of Obedience

Andy concludes, "Listening to God is the most profitable, wise, and healthy thing you can do. It's not just about making good decisions—it's about walking in intimacy with the Creator."

God's voice led Andy and his family through impossible odds to fulfill His promises. His story is a testament to the truth of Matthew 4:4: *"Man shall not live by bread alone, but by every word that proceeds from the mouth of God."*

This chapter is a powerful reminder that God is intimately involved in every detail of our lives, from the grand to the mundane. Whether through Scripture, wise counsel, or supernatural provision, His guidance is sure for those who seek Him.

Summary

Promise: *"Man shall not live by bread alone, but by every word that proceeds from the mouth of God." - Matthew 4:4*

Problem: When the man who committed to buy the house after selling their house, it changed everything for Andy and his wife. Where would the funds come from?

Miracle: God put 5 people's names in his mind that he should reach out to. One of them became the source of funds that were lent to Andy and later totally forgiven.

Jeremiah's Prophetic Act of Faith

In the thirty-second chapter of Jeremiah, we encounter an extraordinary story of faith and obedience. It's a narrative that might seem illogical at first glance but is rich with spiritual applications for believers today. Jeremiah, the prophet of God, is instructed to buy a piece of property in a land that is under siege by the Babylonians. This act, commanded by God, serves as a prophetic declaration of hope and restoration for the people of Israel.

Jeremiah's life was marked by hardship and rejection. As a prophet during one of Israel's most turbulent periods, he delivered messages of impending judgment because of the nation's disobedience. By the time we reach chapter 32, the Babylonian army has surrounded Jerusalem, and the city's fall is imminent. Jeremiah himself is imprisoned by King Zedekiah for prophesying that Judah would be delivered into the hands of the Babylonians.

It is in this dire context that God speaks to Jeremiah, instructing him to purchase a field in Anathoth, a town already under enemy control. The land is being sold by his cousin Hanamel, fulfilling the law of redemption that allowed family members to buy back property to keep it within the clan (Leviticus 25:25).

From a human perspective, buying land in a war zone seems absurd. The property had no practical value at the time; it was occupied by the enemy and would remain so for an indeterminate period. Yet, Jeremiah obeys without hesitation. He meticulously follows the legal procedures of the time, signing the deed, sealing it in a clay jar, and ensuring its preservation.

This act of obedience is more than a simple transaction. It is a prophetic act. Through this seemingly illogical purchase, God is making a statement: "Houses, fields, and vineyards will again be bought in this land" (Jeremiah 32:15). The field represents the promise of restoration, a tangible sign of hope that God's judgment is not the end of the story.

Spiritual Applications for Believers Today

Jeremiah's purchase of the field teaches profound lessons about faith, obedience, and hope:

1. **Faith in God's Promises**
   Jeremiah acted on God's promise, even when circumstances seemed contrary. Believers today are called to trust God's Word, even when His promises seem distant or impossible. Faith is not dependent on visible evidence but on the certainty of God's character and His faithfulness.

2. **Obedience Amid Uncertainty**
   Jeremiah's willingness to obey God's instruction, despite the apparent futility of the act, challenges us to follow God's leading even when we don't understand. Obedience often requires stepping out in faith, trusting that God's plans are higher than ours.

3. **Hope in Restoration**
   The purchase of the field was a declaration of hope. For believers, it's a reminder that God is in the business of restoration. No matter how bleak the situation, God's promises assure us that He can bring beauty from ashes and joy from mourning (Isaiah

61:3).

4. **Prophetic Acts as Witnesses**
   Jeremiah's act was a visible demonstration of God's promise. Similarly, our actions can be prophetic declarations to the world. Living out our faith, showing love in adversity, and investing in God's kingdom are ways to testify to His truth.

Jeremiah's story resonates deeply in today's world. Believers may find themselves in situations that feel like a "Babylonian siege"—whether it's financial difficulties, health challenges, or spiritual battles. Like Jeremiah, we are called to act in faith, holding onto the promises of God.

Consider those who invest in ministries, plant churches, or start businesses in challenging environments. Their actions often seem illogical by worldly standards, yet they reflect a deep trust in God's ability to bring about restoration and growth.

Conclusion

Jeremiah's purchase of the field in Anathoth is more than a historical anecdote; it's a timeless lesson in faith and hope. It reminds us that God's plans often defy human logic but are always aimed at redemption and restoration. As believers, we are invited to participate in His work, acting in faith and obedience, knowing that our trust in Him will never be in vain.

In the face of uncertainty, let Jeremiah's story inspire us to ask: What fields is God asking us to buy today? What prophetic acts of faith can we undertake to declare our trust in His promises? Like Jeremiah, may we be bold in our obedience, confident in the hope of restoration that God promises to His people.

The Bible does not provide an exact timeline for when Jeremiah personally returned to the land he purchased after the Babylonian captivity began. Here's the context:

1. **The Purchase of the Land**: Jeremiah 32 describes how God told Jeremiah to buy a field in Anathoth as a prophetic act to symbolize that there would one day be a return to the land, even though Judah was about to go into Babylonian captivity.

2. **The Exile**: The Babylonian captivity lasted 70 years, as prophesied by Jeremiah himself (Jeremiah 25:11-12). This was a collective period of exile for the people of Judah.

3. **Jeremiah's Fate**: Jeremiah did not go to Babylon with the exiles. Instead, he stayed in Judah for a time and later was forcibly taken to Egypt by a group of Jews fleeing after the assassination of Gedaliah, the Babylonian-appointed governor (Jeremiah 43:5-7). There is no biblical record of Jeremiah ever returning to the land of Israel.

4. **The Land's Restoration**: The fulfillment of the promise symbolized by the land purchase occurred when the exiles returned under leaders like Zerubbabel, Ezra, and Nehemiah, starting around 538 B.C., after the decree of Cyrus the Great (Ezra 1).

In summary, Jeremiah's purchase of the land symbolized hope and restoration, but he himself did not return to see this promise fulfilled. The people of Judah began returning to the land after 70 years of captivity.

Summary

Promise: *"For My thoughts are not your thoughts, nor are your ways My ways," says the* LORD. *"For as the heavens are higher than the earth, so are My ways higher than your ways, And My thoughts than your thoughts. – Isaiah 55:8,9*

Problem: Israel was being taken captive by another nation. Yet God told Jeremiah to buy land in Israel as a prophetic statement to the nation that they would return.

Miracle: *"Houses, fields, and vineyards will again be bought in this land" - Jeremiah 32:15*
And they did return to the land.

Chapter 13: What Does It Mean to Partner with God?

Andy Mason was a former banking professional and offers a compelling insight into what it means to partner with God in our work lives. Through his stories, Andy illustrates the profound impact of bringing God's presence into seemingly secular spaces—even the heart of Wall Street.

Andy shares a pivotal moment when he and his team decided to test the principle of releasing God's peace, as described in Luke 10. In this passage, Jesus sends his disciples into cities, instructing them to declare peace to each house they enter. Andy interprets this peace—or Shalom—as encompassing wholeness in every aspect of life: physical, financial, mental, emotional, and relational. But rather than treating it as a theoretical concept, Andy's team decided to explore its practical application.

They asked a daring question: What if this peace could tangibly transform one of the most anxiety-filled environments in the United States? Their answer led them to the New York Stock Exchange (NYSE).

God's Power at the New York Stock Exchange

Despite having no prior connections to the NYSE, Andy and his team prayed for open doors. Over time, they were granted access for an educational tour. Dressed in suits to fit the formal atmosphere, they entered the trading floor with a unique purpose: to learn, pray, and witness what God might do.

The results were astonishing. Traders experienced physical healings—one man with a fractured C2 vertebra, injured during Hurricane Sandy, regained full mobility and was freed from pain after a prayer on the street outside the NYSE.

Others with chronic pain in their knees and backs also reported complete healing.

But the transformation wasn't confined to physical miracles. The team observed unexpected shifts in the stock market. On their first day there, the Dow Jones saw a 60-point rise. By the end of the week, major indices experienced a 2% increase. While multiple factors influence financial markets, news outlets like USA Today and CNN Money reported that there was no singular catalyst for this growth. Could it be, Andy wondered, that God's peace—released in the marketplace—played a role?

Applying Peace in Crisis

Andy's experiences didn't stop at the NYSE. During a strategic retreat with a global business team, he shared these stories and emphasized the power of releasing peace. One businessman in attendance would soon face an extreme test of this principle.

The next day, his company's servers crashed, leaving them without critical trading information during a high-stakes moment. Anxiety gripped the team, and chaos ensued. But remembering the teaching from Luke 10, the businessman chose a different approach. Instead of panicking, he prayed: "God, I release peace to this house. Let Your peace reign."

As he rode the elevator to the trading floor, a sense of calm washed over him. When he arrived, the atmosphere of panic remained—until a miraculous discovery: one monitor, accidentally left on overnight, still had access to the necessary trading information. The team quickly used it to regain control of the situation. This businessman's decision to partner with God and release peace transformed a potential disaster into a testimony of divine provision.

The Power of Shalom

Andy's stories illustrate a profound truth: partnering with God is an invitation to bring His Kingdom into every aspect of life, including work. Releasing peace, as instructed in Luke 10, is more than a spiritual gesture; it is a declaration of God's presence and provision. This peace can bring healing, clarity, and breakthrough—whether in the marketplace, a boardroom, or a crisis.

So, what does it mean to partner with God? It means embracing the reality that His power is available in every situation. It means stepping out in faith, experimenting with the possibilities of His Kingdom, and declaring His peace over our circumstances. As Andy's journey demonstrates, with God, nothing is impossible.

Summary

Promise: God promises to be our partner in life and business.

> *"He who has My commandments and keeps them, it is he who loves Me. And he who loves Me will be loved by My Father, and I will love him and [a]manifest Myself to him."* – *John 14:21*

Problem: There were various problems revealed when Andy and his team offered to pray for people in the stock exchange.

Miracle: God answered multiple prayers that impacted several lives of those on working on the stock exchange and even the activity of the stock exchange.

David Learned to Partner with God

David is a great example of someone who learned to partner with God. His story begins in the sheep fields of Bethlehem, far from the halls of power and recognition. He was the youngest son in a family that gave him little regard. In fact, scripture hints that David may have been born out of wedlock (Psalm 51:5), which could explain the distance between him and his brothers. Yet, while David may have been overlooked by men, he was never overlooked by God.

It seems his mother saw something different in him—perhaps a divine spark, a glimpse of destiny—and she nurtured it. David learned to play the harp, and as he watched over his father's sheep, he spent countless nights worshiping God under the stars. There, in the solitude of the fields, David developed a devotional life that would shape the rest of his journey. His psalms, written through trials and triumphs, reflect a heart deeply connected to his Creator.

David didn't just know about God; he knew *God.* His relationship with the Lord was personal and passionate. In Psalm 63:1, he wrote, *"O God, you are my God; earnestly I seek you; my soul thirsts for you..."* David's worship wasn't a ritual—it was a lifeline. He danced before the Ark of the Covenant with abandon, unconcerned with public opinion, because his joy was rooted in the presence of the Lord. His psalms are filled with declarations of God's steadfast love, mercy, faithfulness, and strength—attributes David personally encountered.

One of David's earliest public partnerships with God was on the battlefield with Goliath. While Israel's seasoned warriors trembled, David saw the situation through the lens of faith. "You come to me with sword, spear, and javelin," he told the Philistine giant, *"but I come to you in the name of the Lord of hosts." - 1 Samuel 17:45* His boldness came not from arrogance, but from trust in God's power. This was not David acting alone—this was divine collaboration. God gave David both the courage and the victory that day.

Inquiring of God Before Battles

David consistently inquired of God before making strategic decisions, particularly in warfare. Unlike Saul, who often acted presumptuously, David would ask, *"Shall I go up against the Philistines?" -2 Samuel 5:19* And when God said yes, David obeyed—and succeeded. When God said wait, he waited. This sensitivity to God's voice was a hallmark of his kingship. David understood that partnering with God required not just faith, but humility and obedience.

Throughout his reign, David publicly proclaimed that God was the source of his strength, success, and salvation. In 2 Samuel 22:2-3, he declared: *"The Lord is my rock, my fortress, and my deliverer... in whom I take refuge."* He never took credit for the victories—he gave the glory to God. His life was a continual declaration that he was dependent on the Lord for everything.

David was far from perfect. His sins—most notably his affair with Bathsheba and the orchestrated death of her husband, Uriah—had devastating consequences. Yet, what made David different was his heart of repentance. In Psalm 51, we see a broken man pleading for mercy, not defending himself. God could work with such a heart. That's why, even after his failures, God still called him *"a man after my own heart." -Acts 13:22*

David's Partnership with God—In Every Season

From the pasture to the palace, David partnered with God. Whether slaying giants, leading armies, worshiping in the tabernacle, or repenting in sackcloth, he lived with a deep awareness that his life was not his own. He lived *with* God, *for* God, and often *through* God's strength. His story encourages us that true partnership with God is not about perfection—it's about connection.

Summary

Promise: David believed in the God of his ancestors Abraham, Isaac and Jacob. He proclaimed that faith to those around him. Though small in stature, he was large in faith and boldness. He told the Philistine giant, *"but I come to you in the name of the Lord of hosts." -1 Samuel 17:45*

Problem: David was raised in humble beginnings and had to fight his perceived weaknesses in physical size and family history of being a son out of wedlock and not considered a legitimate son of his father Jesse. That is why he was not considered when Samuel the prophet came to choose the next king of Israel.

Miracle: God looks at the heart, not at the physical attributes. God used David to defeat Goliath and many other battles Israel would have. He would become a great king in Israel.

Chapter 14 - When God Makes the Sale

Michael Pink has been a long-time friend. We were both part of the early days of the faith@work movement. Michael's early career was in the sales industry as a copier sales executive. He later transitioned into sales training and ultimately to Christian leadership training. He has authored many books.

I asked Michael to share a supernatural story in the area of sales. He was glad to share a powerful story he experienced in his sales life.

"It was August 1979. I was working as a copier salesman, and our corporate year-end was August 31st. That year, the company set a challenge: make $66,000 in sales over three months and receive a $2,000 bonus. That translated to about thirteen copier sales. But only 15 to 20 percent of the guys ever actually hit that quota in a 90-day period.

For me, June and July had been amazing. By the time August rolled around, I was already at quota. Everything I sold in August would be bonus territory—gravy on the mashed potatoes. To make it even better, we had five weeks in August that year instead of four. Five golden weeks to crush it.

So, I did what I knew to do: I prayed, I gave generously, I sought the Lord with everything I had. 'God,' I said, 'I'm trusting You to partner with me.' I expected favor, results, miracles."

Week 1: Silence

"At the end of the first week—no sales. I was puzzled. I asked the Lord, "What's going on?"His reply was simple: 'Trust Me.' Well, it was still early. I thought, Four weeks left—no big deal. That's like a normal month. I can trust You, God.

Week 2: Still Nothing

Second week—still zero. Now I was getting nervous. I went back to the Lord. "I'm doing everything I know to do, Lord. What's happening?" Again: 'Trust Me.' I tried to shake off the anxiety. Two weeks is a long time in sales. Anything can happen.

Week 3: No Sales, No Prospects

By the end of the third week, still no sales. No leads. No action. My confidence was evaporating. My prayers got more desperate. And God? Still the same: 'Trust Me.' I looked at the calendar. 'Okay,' I reasoned, 'I've still got two weeks. That's like half a month. Many times, I've made all my sales in the second half.'

Week 4: Empty Hands

But after week four—nothing. Zero. Nada. Not even a solid prospect. I was cold calling. Grinding. Pushing. But it felt like I was pushing against a brick wall. By Thursday night of that fourth week, I was beyond stressed. I was on straight commission. I had a wife, kids, a mortgage, a car payment. I was supposed to be in bonus territory, but I was staring at a goose egg.

Week 5: Losing Heart

Monday, Tuesday, Wednesday and Thursday came and went with zero sales, evaporating the last of my hopes as I prepared for Friday, the last day of the month, and our year end. What was I going to do? Nothing left but a goose egg. One of my fellow salesmen noticed the stress on my face and said, 'Can I pray for you?'

'Sure,' I said. I sat down in a chair in the middle of the office, and he laid hands on me and began to pray. I don't remember a single word he said. But I'll never forget what happened next.

The Vision

As he prayed, I saw a movie playing in my mind. In the vision, I was standing in the shallow end of a swimming pool, and Jesus was right next to me. He turned to me and said, *"Hey Michael, how would you like it if I baptized you and held you underwater for 60 seconds—and supernaturally enabled you to breathe?"*

'Lord,' I said, 'That would be fantastic! I hate having to come up for air. It would be amazing to just stay down and inhale.' So, in the vision, Jesus pushed me under the water. I expected to breathe underwater, like He said. But instead, I panicked. I held my breath, kicked, squirmed, and finally came up gasping for air.

And in that moment, I realized: I didn't trust Him. I tried to hold on. I tried to survive. I relied on my own strength. That night, the vision haunted me. I knew I had not truly let go. I said I trusted Him, but I was still holding my breath.

Friday: Letting Go

The next morning—Friday, the final day of the sales year—I woke up with a sense of surrender. 'Lord,' I said, 'I've got eight hours left. Whatever happens today, I trust You. If nothing happens, I'm still Yours. If You do something great, then praise You. But for the first time… I truly let go.' I stopped striving. Stopped pushing. I let go—and I meant it.

The Floodgates Open

The first guy I called on bought a copier. That had never happened before. Then the second guy bought one. Then the third. Then the fourth. By lunchtime, I had made my monthly quota—all in a single morning. But it wasn't over. The fifth guy bought. Then the sixth. Then the seventh. I was in shock.

By late afternoon, I had sold **12** copiers, over $56,000 in sales. I walked into the office at 5:30 p.m., stunned. On the message board, someone had left a note: A prospect was interested in a brochure. I called him. He was still in the office, so I drove over. He bought a $10,000 copier.

Thirteen sales in one day. $66,000 in business. **Exactly the three-month quota… in eight hours!**

A Lesson from the Boat

It reminded me of Peter. Remember when he and the disciples had fished all night and caught nothing? These were professionals. Then Jesus shows up and says, *"Cast your net on the right side of the boat."*

What did they have to lose? They obeyed—and pulled up a catch so big it nearly sank two boats. Peter fell at Jesus' feet, overwhelmed.

That's how I felt. I learned something that day—not about sales, but about trust. I didn't get better at closing. I didn't discover a slick new pitch. God simply did His thing.

And He waited until I let go.

Let Go and Let God

Friend, I want to encourage you. You might be striving, pushing, barely hanging on. You may be trusting God in word, but holding your breath under water.

Let go. Trust Him. Breathe.

Do your part, but let God do what only He can. The results may just astonish you."

Summary

Promise: *"Trust in the Lord with all your heart, and lean not on your own understanding; in all your ways acknowledge Him, and He shall direct your paths." - Proverbs 3:5-6*

Problem: Michael needed to make copier sales in a year-end competition. the company set a challenge: Make $66,000 in sales over three months and receive a $2,000 bonus. That translated to about thirteen copier sales. But only 15 to 20 percent of the guys ever actually hit that quota in a 90-day period.

Miracle: Thirteen sales in one day. $66,000 in business. Exactly the three-month quota… in eight hours.

Divine Strategy: How Jacob Broke Free from Control and Built a Business

Jacob, the third patriarch of Israel, was no stranger to struggle. Born into a lineage rich in destiny but marred by generational strongholds, Jacob carried both the blessing of Abraham and the burden of a family history steeped in manipulation and control. His journey would ultimately become one of the most powerful testimonies of how God partners with a man to bring about supernatural provision and freedom through divine strategy.

After deceiving his brother Esau and securing the birthright and blessing, Jacob fled for his life and took refuge in the home of his uncle Laban. What Jacob didn't realize at the time was that he was stepping into a relationship with a man who mirrored many of his own deceptive tendencies. Laban was a skilled manipulator, a man who understood how to use people for his own gain.

Jacob fell in love with Rachel, Laban's younger daughter, and agreed to work seven years in exchange for her hand in marriage. But true to his nature, Laban tricked Jacob and gave him Leah, the older sister, instead. Jacob was forced to work another seven years for Rachel—the woman he truly loved.

Fourteen years of labor. Fourteen years of being under the thumb of a man who used Jacob's gifts for his own wealth. But God was not finished with Jacob.

Breaking Free from Control

Jacob had served Laban faithfully. In fact, it was because of Jacob's presence and blessing that Laban's flocks had prospered. Yet there came a point where Jacob realized that as long as he remained under Laban's roof and rule, he would never step into the fullness of what God had for him. He had to break free from the control and manipulation.

But how? Laban was clever, and Jacob had few physical assets of his own. It would take a strategy that only God could provide.

It was then that God gave Jacob a divine strategy—one that would seem foolish to the natural mind but proved to be genius. In a dream, Jacob saw an image of the flocks breeding in a specific way that produced spotted, speckled, and streaked sheep and goats—animals that would be identified as his, according to an agreement he made with Laban.

Jacob proposed a new deal: he would continue to care for Laban's flocks, but any sheep or goats that were born speckled or spotted would belong to Jacob, and the rest would remain Laban's. Laban, ever the opportunist, thought it was a clever way to keep the best for himself and agreed to the terms.

But God had another plan.

Jacob implemented what he saw in the dream, placing peeled branches in the watering troughs when the strongest animals came to breed. Miraculously, the offspring were born spotted and speckled. Over time, Jacob's flocks grew stronger, healthier, and more numerous, while Laban's declined.

This was no fluke. This was a download from heaven—a God-given business strategy that enabled Jacob to build wealth and independence.

From Servant to Shepherd Entrepreneur

Jacob's story is a blueprint for anyone who has ever felt stuck under someone else's control or manipulation. He didn't fight Laban with swords or rebellion. He didn't try to take by force what was rightfully his. Instead, he partnered with God. He listened. He obeyed. He implemented a supernatural idea that no one else could have conceived—and it worked.

Jacob's business wasn't built through conventional means. It was birthed in the secret place, through a dream given by God.

His wealth wasn't stolen or inherited; it was created through divine innovation and faith in God's provision.

Lessons for Today

Jacob's journey teaches us several powerful truths:

1. **God sees injustice** – Even when others manipulate or take advantage of us, God is watching, and He will bring justice in His time.

2. **Freedom often requires a step of faith** – Jacob had to step out from Laban's system and trust God for his own provision.

3. **God can give you ideas no one else can see** – Divine strategy can be the key to breakthrough in business, ministry, or personal life.

4. **Prosperity follows obedience** – Jacob acted on what he saw in the dream, and that obedience produced supernatural results.

You may find yourself in a place right now where it feels like someone else holds the reins of your future. Like Jacob, you may be serving faithfully but feel trapped by circumstances or people. Don't despair. Ask God for a strategy. Seek Him for a divine idea. When the time is right, He will give you a vision that leads to freedom and fruitfulness.

The same God who gave Jacob a dream for his sheep business can give you a dream for your destiny.

Summary

Promise: *"Jacob has a dream of a ladder reaching to heaven, which God uses to reaffirm his covenant with Jacob." - Genesis 28:12*

Problem: Jacob felt used by his uncle Laban. He needed a way to free himself from the control and manipulation of his uncle.

Miracle: God gave Jacob a vision for building his own sheep and goat business that would allow him to marry Rachel and leave the employment of Laban.

Chapter 15 - Switzerland UBS Executives Say "Yes" to Jesus

There are moments in ministry when heaven seems to bend low, when God's Spirit moves unexpectedly among people of influence—and one such moment unfolded on a cool evening during a ministry trip I had to Zurich, Switzerland in 2005.

I had arrived in Zurich after a seven-hour overnight flight from New York City. My purpose? To speak to a gathering of top executives from UBS (Union Bank of Switzerland), held within the very walls of their global headquarters—home to over 4,000 employees. The opportunity itself was unusual and sacred.

I had been invited to speak by Aaron Smith, an American hedge fund manager who was part of a small group of financial business leaders and avid TGIF subscribers.

Access to that space had been granted through what could only be described as a series of divine arrangements. As we walked into the presentation room that afternoon to prepare, it felt like stepping into a presenter's dream—state-of-the-art theater-style seating, pristine acoustics, and a massive screen for visuals. One of the team members confided that getting access to this venue was nothing short of a miracle.

Earlier that day, I joined a small prayer gathering hosted by Aaron. A man of deep prayer and discernment, Aaron had carried the vision for this meeting for months, believing God was preparing to move among leaders in the financial sector. At that point, just two weeks before, there had only been 20 RSVPs. But by the time the meeting began, 145 executives had filled the room—many of them high-level executives from UBS and other institutions.

What unfolded that night was something only the Holy Spirit could orchestrate.

While I rarely give salvation invitations in such settings, God had prepared me weeks earlier. At a meeting in Orlando, I had felt impressed to create a simple Gospel PowerPoint slide—though at the time, I had no clear sense of when or where I would use it. As I stood in that UBS auditorium and sensed the openness in the room, I knew it was for this meeting.

At the conclusion of my talk I extended a simple, quiet call to receive Jesus, I invited those in attendance to pray. To my astonishment, around two dozen hands went up—financial executives surrendering their lives to Christ in the heart of one of the world's most powerful banking institutions. It was as if the Spirit of God had slipped into the boardroom and rewritten the agenda.

The next day, a note from one of the attendees, Anne, confirmed the depth of what had taken place. Anne was the wife of a prominent CEO of a multinational company based in Zurich, wrote:

"Os spoke with the clear voice of a prophet... When he spoke of dismantling the spirits of greed and fear 'heart by heart,' I was really encouraged to do exactly this in my daily life... His call to give hearts to Jesus at the end was so powerful, with his quiet manner. Mr. Hillman is an encourager of the most gentle kind—it reminded me of Barnabas in the book of Acts."

Her words echoed what many had felt: the Gospel had come—not with fanfare, but with quiet authority.

From Zurich, I traveled to Bern to continue the ministry. There, I reunited with Jurg Opprecht, a dear friend and pioneering entrepreneur who owns a 5-star hotel in the Alps, is an accomplished abstract artist, and founded the Business &

Professional Network (BPN), a marketplace ministry impacting leaders throughout Switzerland and beyond. Jurg and I both consider Gunnar Olson our mentor, and it was Jurg who had translated *TGIF* into German years earlier, opening doors in the German-speaking world.

That evening, I spoke at a next gen local church where Jurg's son pastors. Around 50 leaders—both business and church—gathered to explore a message new to many of them: that the Church must be equipping workplace leaders, not just traditional ministry leaders. The response was deeply encouraging. Seeds were planted that night for future collaboration.

The next day, I was the keynote speaker for an all-day conference focused on the 7 cultural mountains of influence—business, government, media, arts and entertainment, education, family, and religion. I delivered two 90-minute sessions with the help of an interpreter, though many attendees spoke English. Some had even made the trip from Zurich after attending the UBS event. The gathering was intimate, but full of influencers. These were the gatekeepers of their respective mountains—and many were longtime TGIF subscribers.

On Saturday, I recorded a testimony from Richard Tan, another financial professional and TGIF reader. His story was remarkable. Not only had TGIF helped guide him through his "Joseph journey" in the financial world, but he had also been miraculously healed of a brain tumor. We shared a meal that evening in a historic Bern restaurant, its walls telling stories dating back to 1781.

Sunday provided a breath of rest. I joined Jurg, Benzli, Aaron, and two other leaders for church at the same location I had spoken at earlier. The church was contemporary and vibrant, holding three services each Sunday. That afternoon, we took a scenic drive up into the Swiss Alps to visit Jurg's extraordinary hotel—a 5½-star destination that caters to the "first generation wealth" market, with average room rates over $1,000 per night. The hotel had won "Hotel of the Year" in Switzerland just three years after opening. It was more than a hotel; it was a gallery of Jurg's abstract art and a testament to excellence offered unto God. The view from the Alps reminded me of how high God's plans can reach when submitted to His purposes.

Before returning to the U.S., I had one final meeting—breakfast in Zurich with Aaron, Stephen Gardner of Credit Suisse, and another leader. Stephen, a bold believer who had come to Christ just six years prior, is passionate about sharing the Gospel. He hands out TGIF devotionals by the box and wears a *TodayGodIsFirst* wristband daily as a witness. Our conversation quickly turned to the financial world. As insiders, they confirmed what I've sensed for some time: a global shaking is coming to the financial systems of the world—greater than what we saw in 2008. God is preparing His Josephs, Daniels, and Esthers for such a time as this.

This trip was more than a speaking tour. It was a visible demonstration that God is at work in the upper echelons of the financial world, drawing leaders into His Kingdom—not just to save their souls, but to realign systems. We are watching God raise up Kingdom influencers who will carry His values into boardrooms, investment firms, and nations.

Yes, Jesus visited Zurich. And the bankers said, "Yes!"

Summary

Promise: *And He said to them, "Go into all the world and preach the gospel to every creature. – Mark 16:15*

Problem: Being intimidated by the secular world of big finance.

Miracle: God gave me faith and boldness to step into a situation that was intimidating and saw God touch the hearts of many.

The Power of Preaching that Leads to Salvation

One of the most consistent patterns in Scripture is that when God's word is proclaimed with boldness and truth, it has the power to pierce hearts and lead people to salvation. Preaching was never meant to be a passive activity or mere religious exercise. It is the divine delivery system for transformation—both personal and societal. Throughout Scripture, we see preaching provoke repentance, ignite revival, and call people into covenant with the living God.

Let's look at several biblical moments where preaching led directly to salvation and then draw out timeless principles for effective gospel communication.

Pentecost: Preaching with Power and Conviction (Acts 2:14–41)

It was the day of Pentecost. Peter, freshly filled with the Holy Spirit, stood before a massive crowd in Jerusalem and boldly proclaimed that Jesus—the one they crucified—was both Lord and Messiah. He connected prophecy with reality and called for repentance.

"When the people heard this, they were cut to the heart and said... 'Brothers, what shall we do?'" (v. 37)

Result: 3,000 people gave their lives to Christ and were baptized that very day.

Principle 1: Preach with clarity, boldness, and conviction.
Peter didn't water down the truth. He named sin, exalted Christ, and called people to respond.

The Ethiopian Eunuch: Preaching One-on-One with Relevance (Acts 8:26–39)

Philip met an Ethiopian official reading the prophet Isaiah. When asked about the passage, Philip began with that Scripture and "told him the good news about Jesus."

"Look, here is water! What can stand in the way of my being baptized?" (v. 36)

Result: The eunuch believed, was baptized immediately, and continued on his way rejoicing.

Principle 2: Preach with personal connection and Spirit-led timing.
Philip met the man where he was—spiritually and

intellectually—and brought the gospel right into his moment of seeking.

Cornelius' Household: Preaching that Breaks Barriers - (Acts 10:34–48)

Peter, initially hesitant to associate with Gentiles, obeyed a divine vision and entered the home of Cornelius. There, he shared the gospel of peace through Jesus Christ. *"While Peter was still speaking... the Holy Spirit came on all who heard the message." (v. 44)*

Result: Salvation came to the Gentiles—baptized, filled with the Spirit, welcomed into the Kingdom.

Principle 3: Preach without prejudice—God's message is for everyone.
The gospel isn't limited by culture, background, or history. Peter's willingness to cross lines opened the door for a new era in church history.

The Philippian Jailer: Preaching in a Crisis - (Acts 16:25–34)

Paul and Silas, beaten and imprisoned, sang hymns at midnight. After a supernatural earthquake shook the prison doors open, the jailer cried out in desperation.

"Sirs, what must I do to be saved?" "Believe in the Lord Jesus, and you will be saved—you and your household." (v. 30–31)

Result: The jailer and his entire household believed, were baptized, and rejoiced.

Principle 4: Preach hope in the midst of crisis.
Sometimes the most effective sermons are lived, not just spoken. Their joy in suffering led to his salvation.

Paul in Athens: Preaching to Intellectuals - (Acts 17:22–34)

Paul addressed philosophers in the Areopagus, connecting their cultural beliefs to the truth of the gospel. He presented God as Creator and Judge, and called for repentance in light of the resurrection. *"When they heard about the resurrection... some believed." (v. 32–34)*

Result: While some mocked, others were deeply impacted and followed Paul.

Principle 5: Preach with cultural awareness and theological depth.
Paul didn't condemn their culture; he used it as a bridge to reveal Christ.

Jonah in Nineveh: Preaching Simple Truth with God's Anointing - (Jonah 3:1–10)

Jonah reluctantly preached a simple message of warning to the wicked city of Nineveh. *"Forty more days and Nineveh will be overthrown." (v. 4)*

Result: The entire city—from king to commoner—repented. God relented from sending judgment.

Principle 6: Preach God's message, not just your own.
The effectiveness of Jonah's message wasn't in its eloquence, but in its divine origin. When God anoints a word, hearts respond.

Summary

Promise: *"And Jesus came and spoke to them, saying, "All authority has been given to Me in heaven and on earth. Go therefore and make disciples of all the nations, baptizing them in the name of the Father and of the Son and of the Holy Spirit, teaching them to observe all things that I have commanded you; and lo, I am with you always, even to the end of the age." Amen." – Matthew 28:18-20*

Problem: Not every believer is willing to preach the Gospel or share their faith. However, when they do, God touches the hearts of people.

What Makes Preaching Transformational?

These stories offer us a composite picture of what true Christ-sharing looks like:

- It is Spirit-led, not self-promoted.
- It is Christ-centered, not man-exalting.
- It calls for response, not mere applause.
- It meets people where they are—but never leaves them there.
- It carries heaven's authority, not just human intellect.

In each case, God used flawed yet obedient messengers to deliver a message that changed lives forever. They weren't preaching for popularity, platform, or applause. They preached because they had been commissioned by God.

Miracle: God's promises are often waiting on the other side of someone's obedience to proclaim the truth for someone's life to be transformed by the power of the Gospel.

So, whether you preach to a crowd, a colleague, or a single stranger at a divine appointment, remember—when the gospel is preached in faith, with the Spirit's anointing, salvation is never far behind.

Chapter 16 - The Jewish Cab Driver

I was in Israel for an international conference during a particularly turbulent time in the nation. Bombs were going off, and the country's tourism industry was suffering immensely, down 90%. Hotels were nearly empty, and cab drivers roamed the streets in search of passengers. It was a time of deep uncertainty and struggle for many in Israel.

I arrived a day early for the conference and found myself standing outside my hotel, observing the quiet, almost eerie atmosphere. Suddenly, a man called out to me. "Hey, would you like to see some of Israel?" he asked. He was a cab driver, and his friendly demeanor put me at ease.

"Because of the downturn in tourism, we cab drivers have a lot of time on our hands," he explained. "If you'd like, I can take you around to see some of the sites."

I hesitated at first, unsure if I should take him up on his offer. But there was something genuine about his approach. "My name is Moses," he added with a grin. "You can call out my name in Israel, and half the country will answer!"

His humor broke the ice, and I decided to trust him. We got into his cab, and he began to take me around. As we drove through the streets of Jerusalem and other iconic sites, Moses asked, "Are you a Christian?"

"Yes," I replied.

To my surprise, he said, "I am too." Intrigued, I asked him to share his story.

Moses told me that he was born Jewish and came from a prominent family. His father-in-law was a well-known rabbi and owned one of the largest farms in Israel. He married his daughter. The rabbi was deeply rooted in their Jewish traditions. But despite his heritage, Moses admitted that he went through a period of emptiness and lack of purpose.

"I wasn't finding meaning in my Jewish roots," he said. "I felt lost and didn't know what to do."

One day, while alone in his house, he heard a voice. It was clear and unmistakable: "Go to Christchurch." Startled, Moses thought someone was in the house with him. He checked every room but found no one. A few moments later, the same voice spoke again: "Go to Christchurch."

"I was in shock," Moses recounted. "I knew no one was there, but the voice was real. It wasn't my imagination."

Not knowing what else to do, Moses opened the Yellow Pages and searched for "Christchurch" in Jerusalem. He found a listing for a Christian church by that name and decided to go there. When he arrived, he explained his experience to the people there. They immediately recognized what had happened: God was reaching out to him.

The people at the church shared the gospel with Moses, and that day, he invited Jesus into his life. His decision to follow Christ changed everything. However, it came at a cost. When his father-in-law learned of his conversion, Moses was disowned and forced to leave the family farm. That's how he ended up driving a cab.

"But I have no regrets," Moses said with a smile. "Finding Jesus gave me the peace and purpose I was searching for all my life."

As I listened to Moses' story, I couldn't help but marvel at God's ability to reach people in the most unexpected ways.

Moses' life had been transformed because he was open to hearing and obeying God's voice.

Perhaps you, too, are going through a challenging time. Maybe you feel lost or uncertain about your purpose. I encourage you to be open and attentive to God's voice. He might be trying to reach you in ways you never imagined.

May Moses' story inspire you to listen, respond, and embrace the journey God has for you.

Summary:

Promise: *And as Moses lifted up the serpent in the wilderness, even so must the Son of Man be lifted up, that whoever believes in Him should not perish but have eternal life. For God so loved the world that He gave His only begotten Son, that whoever believes in Him should not perish but have everlasting life. – John 3:14-16*

Problem: Moses was experiencing a life without Christ, which led to purposelessness.

Miracle: God reached out to Moses in a supernatural encounter by letting Him hear the audible voice of God.

Obeying God's Voice in the Midst of Success

In the book of Acts, Philip, one of the early apostles, stands out as a man full of faith and the Holy Spirit. His ministry was thriving as he preached the gospel with boldness and effectiveness. Crowds listened attentively to his teaching, and many came to faith through his powerful witness. By all appearances, Philip was exactly where God wanted him—his success in ministry was evident, and his impact undeniable.

Yet, in the midst of this fruitful season, Philip heard an unmistakable whisper from the Lord: *"Leave this place and go south to the road that goes down from Jerusalem to Gaza."* It was a desert road, a path leading to the unknown. The instruction defied logic. Why leave a flourishing preaching time for an unpromising journey into the wilderness? Still, Philip knew the voice of God and obeyed without hesitation.

As he traveled, he encountered a carriage carrying an Ethiopian eunuch, a high-ranking official serving the queen of Ethiopia. This man was returning home from Jerusalem, where he had been worshiping, and was reading from the scroll of Isaiah. However, the eunuch did not understand what he was reading.

The Holy Spirit prompted Stephen to approach the carriage, and he asked the eunuch, *"Do you understand what you are reading?" The eunuch replied, "How can I, unless someone explains it to me?"* He invited Philip to join the man in his carriage, Philip began to explain the scriptures, showing how they pointed to Jesus as the Messiah.

As the eunuch listened, his heart was opened to the truth of the gospel. When they came upon a body of water, the eunuch exclaimed, *"Look, here is water. What can stand in the way of my being baptized?"* Philip baptized him on the spot, and the eunuch went on his way rejoicing, his life forever transformed. Some believe this was the beginning of the Gospel being brought to Africa.

This encounter illustrates a profound truth: God's plans often transcend human understanding. Philip's obedience led to a pivotal moment in the spread of the gospel, reaching Ethiopia through the life of this one man. It was a divine appointment that would not have occurred had Stephen clung to the comfort and success of his current ministry.

Lessons in Hearing and Obeying God

1. **God's Voice May Interrupt Success:** Philip was in a season of visible fruitfulness, yet God called him away from it. This reminds us that our human definition of success is not always aligned with God's greater purpose. Sometimes, obedience requires stepping away from what seems good to pursue what is best in God's eyes.

2. **Obedience Requires Faith:** Leaving a place of security and stepping into the unknown demands trust. Stephen had no assurances about what awaited him on the desert road. His example teaches us to trust God's guidance even when it leads us into uncertainty.

3. **Divine Appointments Are on the Other Side of Obedience:** Philip's encounter with the Ethiopian eunuch was orchestrated by God. It was through his obedience that the eunuch not only found salvation but also carried the gospel to his African homeland, expanding God's kingdom in ways Stephen could not have foreseen.

4. **Hearing God's Voice Comes Through Relationship:** Philip's ability to hear and discern God's direction was rooted in his deep relationship with the Lord. Like Philip, we must cultivate intimacy with God to recognize His voice amidst the noise of life.

How often do we resist God's voice because it disrupts our plans or pulls us away from success? Philip's story challenges us to surrender our agendas to the Lord's purposes. It calls us to listen intently for His voice and to respond with a resounding "yes," even when His leading seems counterintuitive.

God's plans are always greater than ours. He sees the ripple effects of every act of obedience, and His purposes never fail. May we have the courage, like Stephen, to obey God's voice and trust His wisdom, knowing that our obedience can open doors for others to encounter Him in transformative ways.

Let us always remember: success is not defined by where we are or what we achieve but by our faithfulness to hear and follow the One who leads us.

Summary

Promise: *"Has the LORD as great delight in burnt offerings and sacrifices,*
As in obeying the voice of the LORD? Behold, to obey is better than sacrifice,
And to heed than the fat of rams. 1 Samuel 15:22

Problem: The Ethiopian eunuch needed someone to explain the scriptures to him.

Miracle: The Holy Spirit told Philip to leave his successful evangelistic meeting to go speak to one person on a desert road.

Chapter 17 - A Supernatural Healing

Earlier in the book I told you about a supernatural encounter I had with Bradley Stuart. Bradley had a supernatural healing early in his life. One of the most remarkable stories of faith and healing I have ever heard came from Bradley. Years ago, he shared with me an extraordinary experience from his teenage years that forever changed his life.

Bradley was born with Cerebral Palsy, a condition that presented significant challenges from the start. His entry into the world was fraught with danger, as he nearly lost his life during a breached birth.

A Journey of Miracles and Faith

"My life began with a series of miracles. When I was born, God's hand was evident in keeping me alive. Yet, only a few days later, doctors gave me just two hours to live. Against all odds, I survived, but the challenges were far from over. By the time I was four years old, it became apparent that I was not developing like other children. I could not walk or talk. After many tests and evaluations, I was diagnosed with cerebral palsy. The doctors explained that the part of my brain controlling coordination had been damaged during birth when they used instruments to pull me out.

"There's no total cure," they told my parents. "But a specialized school for children with cerebral palsy might be able to help him learn to walk and talk, although it will be difficult."

My parents, however, had an unshakable faith in God. They had witnessed His miracles at my birth and believed He was not finished with me yet. They trusted that the God who had brought me through so much would continue to carry me through whatever challenges lay ahead.

At the age of four, I started attending a special school for children with cerebral palsy. There, I received occupational therapy to strengthen my coordination and teach me how to balance, stand, and eventually walk—though every step came with difficulty. I also began working with a speech therapist who helped me learn how to communicate clearly.

I practiced typing on a typewriter to strengthen the coordination in my hands. When I started, I could not even hold a pencil or crayon. But through perseverance and the constant support of my family, who faithfully prayed for me, I began to improve. Slowly but surely, my balance, speech, and coordination developed.

As I gained confidence in walking and talking, I became aware that many of my classmates were still in wheelchairs or using crutches. I began to ask myself, *Why do I have to stay in a school for the handicapped when I can walk and talk now?*

The reality is that cerebral palsy affects individuals in different ways. Some children are unable to walk or talk at all, while others may manage with the assistance of walkers or braces. Then, there are those like me—appearing almost normal but with a few remaining weaknesses.

I brought my question to my parents. They took it seriously and prayed about it. Soon, they felt led to meet with the principal of the public school my sister, Colleen, attended. To our relief, the principal was open to giving me a chance.

When I was nine years old, with faith and courage, my parents made the bold decision to transfer me from the cerebral palsy school to the local public school. They believed that Colleen would be able to look out for me and shield me from some of the challenges I was bound to face.

Facing the Challenges of a New Environment

Transitioning to a regular school was far from easy. I was different, and that difference made me a target. I was mocked and bullied by other children who didn't understand my condition. Yet, even in those difficult moments, God was working. Little did I know that these painful experiences were shaping me to minister to others who would one day face rejection.

In my book *Overcoming Rejection*, I share in detail how God brought healing to me through twenty specific challenges of rejection. Those difficult years taught me to rely on Him in ways I never would have otherwise.

I accepted Jesus as my Savior when I was thirteen, but I didn't fully surrender my life to Him until I was eighteen. That moment of surrender marked the beginning of a deeper healing process—one that continues to this day.

Healing did not come in an instant. I went forward for prayer numerous times, hoping for a miraculous transformation, but nothing seemed to change. Some people told me, "You're not healed because you don't have enough faith," while others said, "There must be sin in your life." Their words stung, but I sought God for answers.

One day, as I poured out my heart to Him, He led me to Mark 16:18:
"They will lay hands on the sick, and they will recover."

It was then that I realized the difference between a miracle and a healing. A miracle happens in an instant, but healing can be a slow process. God was working in me over time, and though the changes were often too gradual to notice, they were happening.

Complications from my condition included one leg being shorter than the other, a disparity that required me to wear a built-up orthopedic boot to walk properly. This was my reality until the miraculous events of 1982.

That year, when I was 16 years old, a visiting medical doctor came to my church to share a testimony. This doctor had not only practiced medicine but had also been called by God into a healing ministry. My father attended the morning session, captivated by the doctor's powerful account of how God was working through him to bring physical and spiritual healing. As the testimony unfolded, my father sensed an undeniable prompting from the Lord: "Bring Bradley tonight to the healing service, and I'm going to touch and heal his leg."

Later that evening, with faith ignited, my father brought me to the service. The atmosphere in the church was electric, filled with anticipation and worship. People gathered with a unified hope for God's presence to manifest in a tangible way. As the service progressed, I approached the altar for prayer. With humility and expectancy, I submitted himself to the moment.

What happened next was nothing short of miraculous. As the doctor prayed, my leg began to lengthen—right there in front of everyone. The Lord healed me instantly, correcting the imbalance that had plagued me since birth. For the first time, my legs were of equal length. I no longer needed the special orthopedic boot I had relied on for so many years. It was as though God had not only restored my physical body but also affirmed His power and love in a deeply personal way.

The transformation was immediate and undeniable. On Friday, I had gone to school wearing my orthopedic boot, just as I always had. When I returned to school the following Monday, I walked confidently in a pair of normal shoes. My classmates and teachers couldn't believe their eyes. The change was so dramatic that it became a testimony in itself, opening doors for me to share the goodness and power of God with those who had never believed or even considered such possibilities.

My healing was not just a physical restoration; it was a profound spiritual marker for me and those around me. It served as a beacon of hope and a demonstration of God's active presence in the lives of His children. To this day, my story continues to inspire faith, reminding us that God's miracles are not confined to biblical times. They happen here and now, often when we least expect them, but most need them.

Prophetic Encouragement and Slow but Steady Healing

Over the years, God sent people into my life who gave me prophetic words of encouragement, reminding me of His promises and keeping me moving forward. Sometimes the progress was so slow that I barely noticed any difference. But in those moments, God would send a friend to point out the change and remind me of how far I had come.

Healing is not always a dramatic, one-time event. Sometimes, it is a journey—one step at a time, guided by faith and strengthened by God's promises. And on this journey, God has never left my side.

Today, I stand as a testimony to God's faithfulness. My life has been a journey of overcoming rejection, learning to trust God fully, and experiencing healing in His perfect timing. Though the challenges have been many, the victories have been greater. God's promises truly start with a problem, but they always end with His glory being revealed.

And through it all, He is still writing my story."

Bradley's testimony of supernatural healing illustrates how God's power can transcend human limitations and medical diagnoses. It encourages us to trust in His divine plan, even when the odds seem insurmountable. For Bradley and all who witnessed his miracle of his leg being healed and his continual healing from cerebral palsy, we see firsthand the glory of God and reaffirmed the truth that, with Him, nothing is impossible.

Summary

Promise: *"A spiritual gift is given to each of us so we can help each other. To one person the Spirit gives the ability to give wise advice; to another the same Spirit gives a message of special knowledge. The same Spirit gives great faith to another, and to someone else the one Spirit gives the gift of healing." - 1 Corinthians 12:7-9 NLT*

Problem: Bradley was born with one leg longer than the other and cerebral palsy

Miracle: His father felt God speak to him to take his son to a healing service and God would heal his leg. And He did! God has been healing Bradley of cerebral palsy over many years.

The Power of Obedience and Influence

In the Old Testament, one story stands out as a profound reminder of God's ability to use anyone—regardless of their position or status—to accomplish His purposes. It's the story of a young servant girl, a man named Naaman, and the prophet Elisha. On the surface, it's a tale of healing and obedience, but at its core, it's about the transformative power of faith and the importance of being faithful in whatever role God has placed you.

The Unlikely Messenger

The story begins with a servant girl who had been taken captive from Israel during one of Aram's military raids. She now served Naaman's wife, the commander of the Aramean army. Naaman was a man of great power and influence, a leader respected by his king and his people. However, he carried a burden that no wealth or power could alleviate: he suffered from leprosy.

Leprosy, a disease that isolated its victims and often led to social rejection, was a source of deep shame and despair. For Naaman, it was a stark contrast to his otherwise illustrious life. Yet, it was through this affliction that God orchestrated an unexpected path to redemption.

The servant girl, though seemingly insignificant in her role, possessed something far greater than status: faith in the living God. She said to her mistress, "If only my master would see the prophet who is in Samaria! He would cure him of his leprosy." (2 Kings 5:3)

Her words set into motion a series of events that would not only lead to Naaman's physical healing but also to his spiritual transformation.

The Obstacle of Pride

Naaman, upon hearing the servant girl's suggestion, took her words seriously enough to seek help. With the backing of the king of Aram, he journeyed to Israel, bringing lavish gifts as a token of gratitude. Yet, when he arrived at Elisha's doorstep, he encountered something unexpected.

Instead of a grand ceremony or an elaborate display of divine power, Elisha sent a simple message: *"Go, wash yourself seven times in the Jordan, and your flesh will be restored, and you will be cleansed." - 2 Kings 5:10*

Naaman's pride flared. The Jordan River, a humble and muddy stream, seemed unworthy of his status. He had expected something dramatic—a wave of the prophet's hand, perhaps, or an invocation to heaven. Frustrated and insulted, Naaman prepared to leave in anger.

How often do we, like Naaman, resist God's instructions because they don't align with our expectations? Pride can blind us to the simplicity of God's solutions. Yet, it was in this moment of resistance that Naaman's servants stepped in, gently urging him to reconsider: "My father, if the prophet had told you to do some great thing, would you not have done it? How much more, then, when he tells you, *'Wash and be cleansed'!" - 2 Kings 5:13*

The Breakthrough of Obedience

Their words penetrated Naaman's heart. Humbling himself, he obeyed Elisha's instructions and immersed himself in the Jordan River seven times. On the seventh dip, his flesh was restored, becoming as clean as a young boy's. Not only was he healed physically, but he also experienced a spiritual awakening. Naaman returned to Elisha, declaring, *"Now I know that there is no God in all the world except in Israel." - 2 Kings 5:15*

Through his obedience, Naaman discovered the power of the God of Israel. His healing became a testimony to the nations, all because of the faith and courage of a young servant girl.

Lessons from a Humble Servant

This story is a vivid illustration of how God often works through the most unexpected people and circumstances. The servant girl's role was small by human standards, yet her influence was monumental. Her faith and willingness to speak up changed the trajectory of Naaman's life and brought glory to God.

Here are some key takeaways from her example:

1. **Faith in Action:** The servant girl didn't let her circumstances define her faith. Despite being a captive in a foreign land, she held fast to her belief in God's power and shared it with those around her.
2. **Courage to Speak:** She could have remained silent, fearing rejection or punishment. Instead, she boldly spoke the truth, trusting that God would work through her words.
3. **God Uses the Humble:** In God's kingdom, no role is insignificant. Whether you are a leader like Naaman or a servant girl in his household, God can use you to accomplish His purposes.
4. **The Importance of Obedience:** Naaman's healing hinged on his willingness to humble himself and obey God's seemingly simple instruction. Often, breakthrough comes not through grand gestures but through faithful obedience to God's word.
5. **Her Value to Her Employer Skyrocketed:** She would never be viewed the same after God used her to impact a high ranking official in the government. No doubt she probably got a raise and given more responsibilities.

God's Plan for You

The story of Naaman and the servant girl is a powerful reminder that God's plans are far greater than our understanding. He can use anyone, in any situation, to bring about His purposes. No matter how small or insignificant your role may seem, remember that you are part of a larger story. When you remain faithful and obedient, God can work through you to impact others in ways you may never fully see.

Like the servant girl, may we all have the courage to trust God, speak truth, and faithfully fulfill the roles He has given us. In doing so, we open the door for His transformative power to flow through our lives and into the world around us.

Summary

Promise: *"Now to Him who is* able to do exceedingly abundantly *above all that we ask or think, according to the power that works in us…" - Ephesians 3;20*

Problem: Naaman, a high ranking general in the army had leprosy.

Miracle: The servant girl knew God could heal Naaman through Elisha. And He did.

She risked her reputation by making the suggestion to her employer.

Chapter 18 - When God Shows Up in the Waiting

Recently I did a podcast interview with Charlie Watkins. Charlie shares a powerful personal experience about the value of God-days.

"In 2008, the private media conglomerate where I worked decided to sell all its businesses, including its crown jewel—The Weather Channel. At the time, I was the president of another of the company's ventures, a cloud computing business called Expedient. Like the other businesses, Expedient was prepared and showcased through a typical sale process, with investment bankers orchestrating the efforts.

The sales process was intense but straightforward, and by September, we were ready to close one of the company's largest transactions. On Friday, September 12, 2008, we successfully closed the sale of The Weather Channel. But just three days later, the financial world was turned upside down. On September 15, the credit markets collapsed, halting all other sale processes in their tracks—including ours at Expedient.

At the time, we thought the delay would last a year, maybe two at most. But I was wrong—very wrong. Expedient wouldn't sell for another eleven years. It wasn't until December 2019 that we finally closed the deal.

So, what happened during those eleven years? On paper, the outcome was extraordinary. In 2008, the best deal we were entertaining valued Expedient at $70 million. When we sold it in 2019, the final valuation was $791 million—more than eleven times the earlier figure. The financial transformation alone was astounding.

But the real story isn't just in the numbers; it's in what happened to me during those years of waiting. Those eleven years changed my heart and life in ways that have stayed with me ever since. They taught me a profound lesson about the difference between simply waiting and waiting on the Lord.

Why does God allow delays?

Delays can feel like roadblocks, but in God's economy, they are often bridges to something far greater. Why does God allow delays? I've come to understand that He uses them to shape us, protect us, and prepare us for what's ahead.

Waiting has a way of exposing what's in our hearts. During those eleven years, I wrestled with impatience, doubt, and frustration. I questioned God's timing and even wondered if He had forgotten me. But through it all, He was refining me.

Waiting forces us to confront our dependence on circumstances instead of God. It strips away our illusions of control and teaches us to rely on Him in ways we never have before. Delays reveal the cracks in our faith and give God room to fill those gaps with His grace.

I learned that waiting on the Lord isn't passive—it's an active process of surrender and trust. It's where we grow in perseverance, humility, and faith. As James 1:4 reminds us, *"Let perseverance finish its work so that you may be mature and complete, not lacking anything."* Delays mature us in ways that instant answers never could.

Looking back, I realize that if Expedient had sold in 2008, the deal would have been far smaller and less impactful. The credit market collapse wasn't a random event—it was God's way of protecting us from selling at the wrong time.

Often, we don't see the bigger picture. We're focused on what we want right now, but God sees what we need in the long term. Delays can be His way of shielding us from opportunities that are good but not His best.

The waiting period wasn't just about financial growth; it was about personal growth. In the spring of 2018, just before we sold Expedient, I was promoted to president and CEO of the entire conglomerate. That promotion stretched me in ways I couldn't have imagined. It prepared me for the challenges and responsibilities that came with the eventual sale.

If the sale had gone through earlier, I wouldn't have been ready to step into that role. The delay gave God time to work on me—to deepen my trust in Him, expand my leadership capacity, and align my heart with His purposes.

God's delays are never wasted. They are seasons of preparation, where He equips us for the blessings and challenges ahead.

Through this experience, I also learned the critical difference between waiting and waiting on the Lord.

Waiting, in its most basic form, is an exercise in endurance. It's not about gritting your teeth, pushing through, and surviving the delay. Waiting on the Lord with the Lord is entirely different. It's not just about getting through the season—it's about being transformed in the process.

Waiting on the Lord is active, not passive. It's a time to lean into Him, to seek His presence, and to trust His promises. It's where we allow Him to do His deepest work in our hearts, healing wounds and reshaping priorities.

When we wait on the Lord, our focus shifts from the outcome to the relationship. We stop asking, "When will this be over?" and start asking, "What do You want to teach me in this?"

The Miracle in the Delay

Sometimes, God shows up with an immediate miracle that takes our breath away. But other times, the miracle is in the delay itself. The financial outcome of our sale in 2019 was incredible, but the real miracle was what happened in my heart during those eleven years.

I became a different person—more patient, more trusting, and more in tune with God's voice. The waiting wasn't a detour; it was the plan. And in the end, it turned out to be far more valuable than I could have ever imagined.

So, if you're in a season of waiting right now, I want to encourage you: don't discount what God might be doing. Sometimes, He's working behind the scenes in ways you can't see yet. And sometimes, the waiting itself is where the greatest transformation happens—not just in the outcome, but in your heart.

Looking back, I wouldn't trade those eleven years for anything. They taught me to trust God's timing, to embrace the process, and to recognize that His plans are always worth the wait."

Summary

Promise: *"But those who wait on the LORD shall renew their strength; They shall mount up with wings like eagles, they shall run and not be weary, they shall walk and not faint." Isaiah 40:31*

"And you shall remember the LORD your God, for it is He who gives you power to get wealth, that He may [a] establish

His covenant which He swore to your fathers, as it is this day." – Deuteronomy 8:18

Problem: Inability to sell their company that led to an eleven year delay.

Miracle: Sold company $791 million, instead of asking price of $70 million—more than eleven times the earlier figure but eleven years later.

Lazarus—Raised for Glory

The story of Lazarus's resurrection is one of the most profound accounts in the New Testament. Found in John 11:1-44, it offers a powerful glimpse into Jesus's compassion, His purpose, and His divine authority over life and death. Lazarus and his sisters, Mary and Martha, lived in Bethany, a small village near Jerusalem. They were not only followers of Jesus but close friends. Their home was a place of rest and fellowship for Him. The Scriptures tell us that Jesus loved Lazarus and his sisters deeply, which makes the events of this story even more significant.

The story begins with a crisis. Lazarus became gravely ill, and his sisters were desperate. They sent a message to Jesus, saying, "Lord, the one you love is sick." Their words revealed not only their closeness to Jesus but also their faith in His ability to heal. They expected Him to come immediately and save Lazarus. Surely, the Messiah, who had healed so many strangers, would not delay when one of His dearest friends was in need.

But Jesus's response was unexpected. Upon hearing the news, He said, "This sickness will not end in death. No, it is for God's glory so that God's Son may be glorified through it." Rather than rushing to Bethany, Jesus stayed where He was for two more days. To the disciples, and likely to Mary and Martha, this delay must have seemed baffling, even painful.

Jesus's delay was intentional. He explained to His disciples, "Lazarus is dead, and for your sake I am glad I was not there, so that you may believe." His words pointed to a greater purpose. Jesus knew that Lazarus's illness and death would serve as a stage for God's glory to be revealed. This would not just be a healing—it would be a resurrection.

During the delay, Lazarus passed away. By the time Jesus and His disciples arrived in Bethany, Lazarus had been in the tomb for four days. In Jewish culture, the fourth day marked the point when death was considered final and irreversible. Any hope of revival was gone. The scene was filled with mourning; friends and neighbors had come to console Mary and Martha. Their grief was raw and palpable.

As Jesus approached Bethany, Martha went out to meet Him. Her words were filled with both faith and sorrow: "Lord, if You had been here, my brother would not have died." Yet, even in her grief, she expressed hope: "But I know that even now God will give You whatever You ask."

Jesus responded with a profound declaration: "Your brother will rise again." When Martha mentioned the future resurrection, Jesus clarified, "I am the resurrection and the life. The one who believes in Me will live, even though they die; and whoever lives by believing in Me will never die. Do you believe this?" Martha affirmed her faith, acknowledging Jesus as the Messiah.

Mary, too, came to Jesus, overwhelmed by grief. She fell at His feet and echoed her sister's words: "Lord, if You had been here, my brother would not have died." Seeing her weeping, and the mourning crowd, Jesus was deeply moved. The shortest verse in the Bible, *"Jesus wept." -John 11:35,* reveals His profound compassion. He shared in their sorrow, even though He knew what was about to happen.

Jesus Raises Lazarus

Jesus went to the tomb, a cave with a stone laid across its entrance. He instructed them to remove the stone. Martha hesitated, pointing out that there would be a terrible odor after four days. Jesus reminded her, "Did I not tell you that if you believe, you will see the glory of God?"

The stone was removed, and Jesus prayed aloud, thanking the Father for hearing Him. He prayed for the benefit of the onlookers, so they would believe that He was sent by God. Then, with a loud voice, He called out, *"Lazarus, come out!"*

To everyone's amazement, Lazarus emerged from the tomb, still wrapped in burial cloths. Jesus instructed them to *"Take off the grave clothes and let him go."* Lazarus was alive. The miracle was undeniable.

The raising of Lazarus caused many to believe in Jesus. It was a powerful testament to His identity as the Son of God. However, it also intensified opposition from the religious leaders. They saw this miracle as a threat and began plotting to kill Him. In their eyes, Jesus's growing influence endangered their authority and the fragile peace with the Romans.

Why Did Jesus Wait?

The delay in Jesus's response to Lazarus's illness was not a sign of indifference but a demonstration of divine purpose. There were three key reasons for the delay:

1. **To Demonstrate God's Glory:**
   By waiting until Lazarus had been in the tomb for four days, Jesus ensured there would be no doubt about the miraculous nature of his resurrection. The timing removed any possibility of natural explanations, magnifying God's glory.

2. **To Strengthen Faith:**
   Jesus's delay provided an opportunity to deepen the faith of His disciples, Mary, Martha, and the onlookers. He said, *"For your sake, I am glad I was not there, so that you may believe."* This miracle was not just about Lazarus; it was a revelation of God's power and Jesus's mission.

3. **To Reveal His Power Over Death:**
   The resurrection of Lazarus foreshadowed Jesus's own death and resurrection. It was a sign that He had authority over life and death, affirming His identity as the resurrection and the life.

The story of Lazarus is more than a historical account; it is a message of hope and power for all believers. It reminds us that God's delays are not denials. His timing is perfect, even when we cannot understand it. Through the resurrection of Lazarus, Jesus demonstrated that He is the source of life, the conqueror of death, and the One in whom we can place our ultimate trust.

As we reflect on this story, we are invited to believe in the One who turns mourning into joy, who calls us out of darkness, and who offers eternal life to all who trust in Him. Like Lazarus, we too can experience resurrection—both in this life and in the life to come.

Summary

Promise: *"This sickness will not end in death. No, it is for God's glory so that God's Son may be glorified through it." – John 11:4*

Problem: He has been dead four days.

Miracle: Jesus raised Lazarus from the dead.

Chapter 19 - Faith in a $400 Billion Company

In 2000, Steve Jobs approached Ron Johnson with a daunting mission: to create Apple's retail stores from scratch. At the time, Johnson was Apple's Vice President overseeing the Americas and Asia Pacific regions. He had one of the best roles at Apple—a position that allowed him autonomy while maintaining Jobs' trust. But this new assignment would require more than his Harvard Business School training or his years in the corporate world. It would require a vision rooted in his faith.

Ron Johnson and John Brandon, another Apple executive, brought their Christian values into the design and operation of what would become the most successful retail stores in history. They wanted to do more than sell products—they wanted to enrich lives.

Enriching Lives Through Retail

"The mission was never about making money," Johnson reflected. "We came down to two simple words: enrich lives."

This guiding principle shaped every aspect of the Apple Store experience. Walking into an Apple Store, customers see two primary elements: people and products. The stores were intentionally designed to remove anything that might distract from these connections.

"The design was to connect people," Johnson explained. "People come to the Apple Store because they love the relationship they have with the employees. It's deep, it's personal. That employee isn't just looking into your wallet; they're looking into your heart. They're trying to make your life a little better."

For Ron Johnson and John Brandon, their faith wasn't just a private matter or something reserved for Sundays. It was the foundation of their approach to work and leadership. Their example challenges us to consider how we can bring our faith into our work-life calling.

Faith at work doesn't necessarily mean overt evangelism or preaching—it means living out values like integrity, service, and love in tangible ways. It means asking questions like:

- How can my work reflect God's love?
- How can I serve others through my skills and influence?
- Am I using my platform to make a positive difference in people's lives?
- How can God solve a problem through me for my employer or my business

Making Love Visible Through Work

Johnson often asked himself, "How do you make love visible through work?" This question became his compass. At Apple, he answered it by creating stores that focused on relationships and service.

When customers visit an Apple Store, they don't just receive a product—they experience care, attention, and problem-solving. The Genius Bar, for instance, isn't merely a technical support station. To Johnson, it was a place of restoration.

"When I see someone getting help at the Genius Bar, I see a relationship being restored," he explained. "That's love made visible."

This approach reminds us that our work—no matter the industry—can be a ministry when it serves others. Whether we're solving problems, offering guidance, or creating solutions, our efforts can reflect God's love.

Living Out Biblical Principles in the Workplace

John Brandon took a similar approach by embedding biblical values into Apple's sales culture. He introduced a set of principles called "Baby's Rules of Success," which became a guide for employees navigating ethical challenges.

"Sales in its essence is being a servant," Brandon said. "You're serving that person to understand them deeply enough to say, 'I can help you.'"

These principles weren't labeled as "Christian" in name, but they embodied values like honesty, humility, and service. Employees carried them on their badges, internalizing the idea that their work had a greater purpose than just generating revenue.

This demonstrates an important truth: you don't have to wear your faith on your sleeve to make an impact. By living out biblical principles, you can influence others in subtle yet powerful ways.

Faith at Work: A Mission, Not Just a Job

Both Johnson and Brandon viewed their roles at Apple as callings, not just jobs. This perspective influenced how they approached their work.

"When Steve hired me, he wanted me to help change the sales culture," Brandon said. "I came in and said, 'Alright, I'll change it, but I'm going to do it my way.'"

For Brandon, that meant relying on his faith to guide decisions, build trust, and create a positive culture. It also meant being intentional about relationships, including his interactions with Steve Jobs.

"Steve was one of the most intentional people I've ever met," Brandon shared. "In his last years, he was very deliberate about where he spent his time and how he left his mark. Many of us had the chance to pray for him and encourage him during that time."

This intentionality mirrors the biblical command to "love your neighbor as yourself." At work, our "neighbors" are our colleagues, customers, and clients. When we approach them with love and service, we reflect God's heart.

Practical Steps to Live Out Faith at Work

Here are a few practical ways to express your faith in your work-life calling:

1. **Excellence in Your Work:** Strive to do your best in every task, knowing that your work reflects your character and your faith.

2. **Integrity in Decisions:** Make ethical choices, even when it's difficult. Stand firm in your values, trusting God to honor your faithfulness.

3. **Service to Others:** Look for opportunities to serve, whether it's helping a coworker, mentoring a junior employee, or going the extra mile for a customer.

4. **Compassion in Relationships:** Treat others with kindness and respect, valuing their dignity and worth.

5. **Prayer for Your Workplace:** Pray regularly for your colleagues, leaders, and the organization. Ask God to

use you as a light in your workplace to manifest His life in the work you do.

A Legacy of Service

The ultimate goal for both men was to hear the words, "Well done, good and faithful servant." They believed that success in business wasn't about power, wealth, or influence—it was about faithfulness to the task God placed before them.

"The Lord decides where He places us," Brandon said. "Whether it's running a business, serving customers, or designing a store, it's all about people. And God is in the people business, so we should be too."

Through their faith-driven approach, Ron Johnson and John Brandon didn't just create retail stores—they created spaces where lives were enriched, relationships were restored, and love was made visible. Their story challenges each of us to ask: How can we bring our faith into our work and use our calling to make a difference for God's Kingdom?

Summary

Promise: "*Now to Him who is able to do exceedingly abundantly above all that we ask or think, according to the power that works in us, to Him be glory in the church by Christ Jesus to all generations, forever and ever. Amen." - Ephesians 3:20*

Problem: Ron Johnson and John Brandon were tasked by Steve Jobs to create an intentional and creative store experience that engaged the customer that made them feel welcomed.

Miracle: Ron Johnson and John Brandon allowed God to guide them to reflect the Gospel in creating new stores for Apple.

Bezalel: A Spirit-Filled Craftsman for God's Glory

The story of Bezalel, a master craftsman of the Old Testament, is one of the most compelling examples of how God calls individuals to use their unique talents for His glory. Bezalel was no ordinary artisan. He was the first person in scripture explicitly described as being "filled with the Spirit of God" for the purpose of artistic craftsmanship. His story teaches us that God values creativity and has given each of us gifts to serve His purposes.

The Call of Bezalel

In Exodus 31:1-6, God instructs Moses to appoint Bezalel, saying: "See, I have chosen Bezalel son of Uri, the son of Hur, of the tribe of Judah, and I have filled him with the Spirit of God, with wisdom, with understanding, with knowledge and with all kinds of skills—to make artistic designs for work in gold, silver and bronze, to cut and set stones, to work in wood, and to engage in all kinds of crafts."

This divine appointment highlights the significance of Bezalel's role in crafting the Ark of the Covenant, the Tabernacle, and other sacred furnishings. These objects were not merely functional; they were artistic expressions of worship, designed to reflect the holiness and majesty of God.

Bezalel's work required not only skill but also spiritual insight. His craftsmanship was an act of worship, demonstrating that God's Spirit empowers us to excel in our work, whether it is building, teaching, creating art, or serving in any other capacity.

The Role of Creativity in God's Kingdom

God's first act in scripture is an act of creation. Genesis 1:1 states, *"In the beginning, God created the heavens and the earth."* As beings made in His image, we are designed to be creators as well. Whether through painting, writing, building, or problem-solving, our creativity reflects the divine nature.

Jesus Himself was a carpenter, working with His hands to build and repair. This earthly vocation reminds us that no work is insignificant when done for God's glory. Proverbs 22:29 emphasizes this truth: *"Do you see someone skilled in their work? They will serve before kings; they will not serve before officials of low rank."* Excellence in our craft can open doors to influence and provide opportunities to share the Gospel.

The story of Bezalel reminds us that God has uniquely gifted each of us. Some are called to serve in the arts, creating beauty that points to the Creator. Others are called to business, teaching, engineering, or medicine. No matter the field, God calls us to use our skills to advance His Kingdom.

In Ephesians 2:10, Paul writes, *"For we are God's handiwork, created in Christ Jesus to do good works, which God prepared in advance for us to do."* Just as Bezalel was equipped for a specific purpose, we too are equipped to fulfill the good works God has planned for us.

Bezalel's story teaches us that excellence matters to God. When the Tabernacle was built, God's instructions were precise, and the craftsmanship had to meet His exact standards. This attention to detail was not about perfectionism but about honoring God through the work.

Colossians 3:23-24 reminds us, *"Whatever you do, work at it with all your heart, as working for the Lord, not for human masters, since you know that you will receive an inheritance from the Lord as a reward. It is the Lord Christ you are serving."*

When we pursue excellence in our work, we glorify God and bear witness to His transformative power in our lives.

Bezalel's story also includes the mentorship of others. God appointed Oholiab to assist him and gave skills to other artisans to contribute to the work. This collaboration underscores the importance of raising up and equipping the next generation to use their gifts for God's purposes.

As stewards of the gifts God has given us, we are called to mentor and encourage others. By sharing our knowledge and skills, we can inspire creativity and help others discover their divine purpose.

Conclusion

Bezalel's life demonstrates that God values creativity and calls us to use our talents to serve Him. Whether you are an artist, a carpenter, a teacher, or a businessperson, your work matters to God. When done with excellence and a heart of worship, your craft becomes a reflection of His glory.

Like Bezalel, let us seek to be filled with the Spirit of God, using our gifts to create, inspire, and build His Kingdom on earth. In doing so, we fulfill the purpose for which we were created and bring honor to the Creator of all things.

Summary

Promise: God wanted an ark to hold the sacred Ten Commandments. He wanted the ark to be designed specifically by Bezalel.

Problem: Moses needed a very skilled craftsman. God knew it was Bezalel.

Miracle: Bezalel did not need a miracle to design the Ark of the Covenant. He simply needed to express the gifting God had given him to design the Ark through the power of the Holy Spirit working in and through him.

Chapter 20 -The Man Who Laid Down His Clarinet

Martin Powell's journey began with the pursuit of musical greatness—and he achieved it. By the age of 20, Martin had fulfilled nearly every ambition he had ever dreamed of. He studied at the prestigious Royal Academy of Music in London, where he won every major prize available—a feat never before accomplished. As a world-class clarinetist, Martin performed 23 world premieres across major cultural centers such as Rome, Paris, and Munich. He even premiered a piece written in honor of Queen Elizabeth II.

But just as his star was rising, Martin had a life-altering encounter. One night, Jesus appeared to him in a dream with a simple but profound ultimatum: *"This is your last chance. You must choose—will you work for My enemy, or will you work for Me?"* In that moment, Martin chose Jesus, stepping away from the trajectory of international fame to follow a far less predictable path—a life led entirely by divine instruction.

At just 25 years old, Martin laid down his clarinet, the hardest thing he'd ever done, and followed God's prompting to buy a music shop in London. He had no money—in fact, he was in debt—but God miraculously provided the means to purchase a three-story building. The shop, aptly named *Talents Music*, became more than just a business. It was a haven for the presence of God, where Martin and his team prayed for one hour each day over every customer who would walk through the doors.

And the Spirit moved. One memorable day, June Ham, a backup singer for George Michael, came in to buy a keyboard. Martin told her, "No, you haven't come to buy an M1 keyboard. You've come to give your life to Jesus." She burst into tears and surrendered her heart right there in the shop. This was not an isolated event—salvations were common in *Talents Music.* As the salvations increased, Martin felt led to start a church above the shop, where new believers could grow in their faith.

God had also gifted Martin with remarkable faith, which led to miraculous answers to prayer. When a friend needed a quality violin she couldn't afford, Martin boldly asked God for a Stradivarius made in the instrument maker's best year. Miraculously, she was given one—exactly as he had prayed.

Martin also walked in obedience and holiness, often using spiritual discernment and even biblical casting of lots to keep his staff and space clean before God. When sin was discovered in his shop, it was confronted and dealt with, reinforcing Martin's belief that God could bless only what was consecrated to Him.

In 2010, Martin moved to the United States, believing God was calling him to a new season. After a lengthy process, he secured his green card in 2010 and settled in Fort Mill, South Carolina. Each week, he asked God what to do next. The answer remained consistent: *"I want you to make money."*

Eventually, God revealed what He meant. Drawing on the biblical symbolism of silver—*keseph* in Hebrew and *argyros* in Greek—Martin began producing silver coins branded as "Talents," a nod to both his former music business and the biblical parable of stewardship. Remarkably, the Hebrew word for "talent" means "round."

A prophetic encounter confirmed the vision. While praying on a mountaintop in Moravian Falls, a man told Martin that a new global economy was coming, one based on the "talent." Unaware of Martin's work, the man had unknowingly affirmed what God had already started through him.

Today, Martin's silver "talents" have been distributed to every continent, part of a movement to help believers steward wealth and prepare for uncertain times. His business, *Kingdom Talents*, is headquartered inside MorningStar Ministries in Fort Mill, where Martin continues to pour out both spiritual and literal silver into the world.

God's commissioning didn't stop there. One day, the Lord asked Martin to write a book on prosperity. Initially reluctant, due to British cultural discomfort with discussing money, Martin eventually agreed. The result was *Money Matters in My Kingdom*, a biblically grounded exploration of God's heart for provision. Rick Joyner, founder of MorningStar, endorsed it as the best book he had ever read on money, Christian or secular.

From international stages to prophetic dreams, music shops to silver mints, Martin Powell's life is a testimony of radical obedience, unwavering faith, and divine provision. He continues to live a salary-free life, relying solely on God's direction and provision, as he builds the Kingdom through wealth and worship.

Summary

Promise: God challenged Martin to give his life fully to the Lord. If he did, God would use him in great ways to build His Kingdom.

Problem: God instructed Martin to lay down his career as a musician. Where would his income come from?

Miracle: God provided supernaturally for Martin as he learned to obey the voice of God in his life.

Faithful Stewardship — Investing What God Entrusts to Us

Jesus told a powerful story in Matthew 25:14–30 known as the *Parable of the Talents*. On the surface, it's a story about a master who entrusts his wealth to his servants. But within this simple tale lies a profound message about how God expects His followers to handle money, abilities, time, and influence. It is one of the clearest pictures in Scripture of how our lives are not our own—we are stewards, entrusted with something sacred.

In the parable, a wealthy master prepares to go on a long journey. Before leaving, he calls three of his servants and distributes his wealth among them—five talents to one, two to another, and one to the third—each according to their ability.

A *talent*, in Jesus' day, was not a small coin. It was a significant sum of money, equivalent to approximately 20 years' wages for a laborer. In modern terms, each talent could be considered worth over a million dollars. This was no small loan—it was a serious investment.

The master was not arbitrary. He gave different amounts based on what he believed each servant could handle. This reveals something about God's nature. He entrusts us with resources according to our capacity—not to burden us, but to match His provision with our potential.

Using the Talents

While the master was away, the servants with five and two talents invested wisely and doubled what they had been given. But the servant with one talent, fearing the possibility of failure, buried his portion in the ground.

This speaks directly to the heart of stewardship: What are we doing with what we've been given? It's not about how much we start with, but what we do with it. God doesn't require equal results—He expects faithful effort.

When the master returned, he praised the two servants who multiplied their talents: *"Well done, good and faithful servant. You have been faithful with a few things; I will put you in charge of many things."*

But the servant who buried his talent was rebuked and called wicked and lazy. His talent was taken and given to the one with ten.

The lesson is clear: God expects a return on what He entrusts to us. Not in a legalistic way, but in a way that reflects trust, faith, and action. Faithfulness means taking risks for the Kingdom.

Stewardship in Today's World

Many believers mistakenly believe stewardship only means managing money conservatively—paying bills, giving a tithe, and avoiding debt. While those are important, biblical stewardship is far more dynamic. It's about recognizing everything we have—money, time, influence, skills, and relationships—as tools for Kingdom impact.

In today's world, a "talent" might look like:

- A thriving business that can bless others and support ministry
- A creative gift used to inspire and bring hope
- Financial resources invested in advancing the Gospel
- Time and energy poured into discipling others
- Platforms and influence used to speak truth and love

God is not asking us to play it safe. He is looking for faithful risk-takers who will leverage what they've been given for His purposes.

At the heart of this parable is a shift in mindset—from ownership to stewardship. What you have is not ultimately yours. Your career, your bank account, your investments, your home, your time—it all belongs to God. You are a manager, not the master.

Paul writes in 1 Corinthians 4:2: *"Now it is required that those who have been given a trust must prove faithful."* The question we must ask ourselves is not "What do I want to do with what I have?" but rather, "What does God want me to do with what He has given me?"

The Faithful Steward's Reward

Faithful stewards are not driven by fear of failure but by love for the Master. They understand that life is short, and eternity is long. They long to hear those words at the end of their journey: *"Well done, good and faithful servant."*

The reward is not only joy in this life, but greater responsibility and joy in the life to come. God's economy operates on trust and faithfulness. When He sees that we are trustworthy with small things, He entrusts us with more.

Reflection Questions:

1. What has God entrusted to me that I may be underutilizing or hiding?
2. Am I managing my money and resources with an eternal mindset?
3. What step can I take this week to invest what I've been given into Kingdom purposes?

Summary

Promise: *"And you shall remember the LORD your God, for it is He who gives you power to get wealth, that He may [a] establish His covenant which He swore to your fathers, as it is this day." - Deuteronomy 8:18*

Problem: Three people were entrusted with various amounts of talents. Two of them did well with their talents, one failed to use their talents wisely. *"Now it is required that those who have been given a trust must prove faithful." – 1 Corinthians 4:2*

Miracle: God asks us to engage with him to multiply our talents by hearing and obeying his voice and using our skills to multiply what we have been entrusted.

Chapter 21 - $150,000 Step of Faith

It was 2017 when I sensed the Lord stirring something bold in my spirit—a call to host an international conference on the seven cultural mountains of influence, right in the heart of Washington, D.C.

Immediately, fear crept in. "Lord, I'm too old to pull this off," I reasoned. I was 65-years old. "What if it fails? I can't afford a major financial loss at this stage in my life."

The idea felt overwhelming, and yet the prompting wouldn't go away.

Soon after, I was invited to speak at a marketplace conference in Bend, Oregon. It was there that I met James and Anna, a couple who, like me, had a background in marketing and a passion for transforming culture through the seven mountains. When I shared my vision, they embraced it with great enthusiasm and offered to be my marketing partner. But there was a caveat: *they couldn't take the financial risk.*

That meant I would be taking it all.

I knew the endeavor would cost at least $100,000 to produce. In the end, the total cost exceeded $150,000. Yet the vision God had given me was crystal clear: bring together major thought leaders for each of the seven mountains—family, arts & entertainment, business, church, education, media, and government—and pair them with a panel of influencers in the same domain. The format would span 3½ days of strategic dialogue and inspiration.

I also believed we should partner with the Museum of the Bible, operated by the Green family, founders of Hobby Lobby. When I reached out to Steve Green, he enthusiastically supported the idea. That confirmation gave me the faith I needed to move forward. It was the boldest step of faith I had ever taken.

The Culture Shapers Summit Becomes a Reality

The final speaker lineup was a who's who of cultural leadership:

- Tony Perkins for the Family Mountain
- Roma Downey for Arts & Entertainment
- Steve Green for Business
- A.R. Bernard for the Church
- Del Tackett for Education
- Hugh Hewitt for Media
- Ken Blackwell for Government

Each keynote was followed by a panel of four leaders who brought depth and perspective from their respective spheres. Over the course of the conference, we hosted 54 different presentations. It was a massive undertaking—and by God's grace, a tremendous success.

My heart was to mobilize attendees into strategic action groups by mountain, using an app we had planned to unveil. This tool would allow them to stay connected and collaborate after the event. While the conference met every expectation in terms of turnout and engagement—and even ended slightly in the black financially—there was one major setback.

The technology app tool wasn't ready.

This deeply disappointed me. I had hoped this would be the springboard for sustained collaboration and movement. Instead, I felt as though I had once again hit the *death of a vision.*

Over the next year, I sought the Lord for the next steps. But progress on the technology stalled. I had already experienced a prior setback when I teamed up with a wealthy business leader who shared a vision for cultural transformation. I invested two years and much relational capital into that effort, only to watch it unravel when he veered off course. Once again, I felt I had little fruit to show for the time and energy expended.

Then something unexpected happened.

A Prophetic Dream: The Battering Ram

About 18 months later, my intercessor Sharon called and shared a vivid dream she had just had:

"You and I were having a casual cup of coffee when some people nearby invited us to join their meeting. It was a gathering of leaders from business, government, and the church. They began asking you for advice and invited you to get involved. Suddenly, these three groups came together and formed a massive battering ram—like the kind used in ancient times to break down fortress doors.

They marched together toward enormous prison gates, and with a single, forceful blow, those gates were shattered. God said, 'I want to release the prisoners and set the captives free in the prison system. But it will require the unity of business, government, and the church to break down these doors.'"

Sharon continued:

"You didn't initiate this. You weren't trying to lead. You were just having coffee. But suddenly, you were called into leadership. You had the calm and clarity to pull all the pieces together. There was such power when those three forces united. I believe God is positioning you for a strategic fathering role in the nation—one of divine authority."

A Glimmer of the Vision Realized—Yet Not Fulfilled

Ironically, just before that dream, I had already been approached by a group with a similar vision to mobilize business, government, and church leaders to impact the seven mountains. They told me they had the funding committed to implement my strategy. I agreed to help, and once again invested time, effort, and influence. But again, the vision fell short—this time due to lack of funding and mobilization. Those who made that financial commitment backed out.

So why did God allow these promising starts only to end in disappointment?

I cannot fully answer that. But I do know this: I was obedient to the call. The outcomes belong to God. Obedience is our part. Results are His.

What About You?

What is God asking *you* to do that requires faith?

Sometimes faith is spelled **R-I-S-K**. Stepping into the unknown, carrying the weight of vision without guarantee of success, and choosing to trust God anyway. The priest could have lost the Ark of the Covenant when they stepped into the Jordan River during flood stage. But God parted the waters and allowed them to walk on dry land.

When we stand before the Lord one day, our desire will be to hear, "Well done, good and faithful servant."

So today, choose obedience. Take the risk. Step into the unknown. For it's often in the *problem* that God births His promise.

Faith That Moves Mountains Begins with a Problem

"Now faith is the substance of things hoped for, the evidence of things not seen." — Hebrews 11:1

We have established that every promise of God begins with a problem. Whether it was an enemy army, an impossible diagnosis, or a barren womb, the setup for a miracle is always a challenge. But the bridge between the problem and the promise is one word: faith.

Faith is an integral part of realizing the solution to our problems. It is not an escape from adversity—it's the pathway through it. And not just any kind of faith, but a biblical, tested, mountain-moving faith that anchors itself in God's voice and acts with boldness even when the outcome is unseen.

What Is Biblical Faith?

In today's culture, faith is often reduced to wishful thinking. But biblical faith is different—it is a conviction birthed from a revelation. Faith is rooted in what God has said, not in how things appear.

"So then faith comes by hearing, and hearing by the word of God." — Romans 10:17

Faith isn't just belief—it's obedient belief that takes God at His word and acts accordingly. It sees the invisible, hears the inaudible, and believes the impossible.

Faith Always Faces a Problem

Let's explore how God's promises were revealed through problems—and how faith was the key to unlocking them.

1. Abraham: The Problem of Barrenness

Abraham and Sarah faced the impossible—they were promised descendants as numerous as the stars, yet were childless in old age. The problem was clear. But faith didn't deny the problem; it rose above it.

"Without weakening in his faith, he faced the fact that his body was as good as dead... Yet he did not waver through unbelief."— Romans 4:19–20

The Promise: Isaac, the child of promise.
The Problem: Infertility and old age.
The Miracle: Believing despite physical impossibility. Birth of Isaac in Sarah's old age.

2. Moses: The Problem of Oppression

The Israelites were enslaved by Egypt for 400 years. God raised up Moses, who, by faith, returned to Egypt and confronted Pharaoh.

"By faith he left Egypt, not fearing the king's anger; he persevered because he saw him who is invisible." — Hebrews 11:27

The Promise: Deliverance and a land flowing with milk and honey.
The Problem: A powerful oppressor.
The Miracle: Speaking God's word to power and trusting God's might over Pharaoh's might. Deliverance of Israel from slavery.

3. Joshua: The Problem of Impenetrable Walls

Jericho's walls represented the first major obstacle in the Promised Land. There was no military strategy to conquer such a fortress. The solution? Worship and obedience.

"By faith the walls of Jericho fell, after the army had marched around them for seven days." — Hebrews 11:30

The Promise: Possessing the land.
The Problem: Humanly impenetrable defenses.
The Miracle: Obeying God's illogical strategy and seeing the walls fall down after

4. David: The Problem of a Giant

David's story starts in obscurity and ascends through adversity. One defining moment: a shepherd boy facing a battle-hardened warrior.

"The Lord who delivered me from the paw of the lion and the paw of the bear will deliver me from the hand of this Philistine."— 1 Samuel 17:37

The Promise: Destiny as king.
The Problem: A mocking giant blocking the path.
The Miracle: Trusting God's past faithfulness in present danger Defeating Goliath. Becoming a King.

5. The Woman with the Issue of Blood: The Problem of Prolonged Suffering

After twelve years of physical, emotional, and financial suffering, this unnamed woman fought through the crowd to touch Jesus.

"Daughter, your faith has made you well. Go in peace." — Luke 8:48

The Promise: Healing and restoration.
The Problem: A hopeless medical condition.
The Miracle: Reaching for Jesus in desperation and trust. She is healed.

When God Allows the Problem, He's Preparing the Promise

Every miracle in Scripture follows a pattern:

1. A Problem that human strength cannot fix
2. A Promise that requires divine intervention
3. A person who walks in faith despite the tension to receive a Miracle.

That's the message of this book. God's promises are not just declarations to be believed—they are invitations to walk by faith when the journey is difficult, unclear, and even painful.

What Does It Take to Walk in Faith?

To experience the kind of miracles seen in Scripture, here's what is required:

1. Hearing God's Voice
You must know what God has spoken. True faith is anchored in a **rhema** word.

2. Obedience in Uncertainty
Faith isn't faith until it's tested. You may have to obey when it doesn't make sense.

3. Perseverance through Delays
Most faith journeys include waiting. Abraham waited 25 years. Joseph waited 13.

4. Refusing to Doubt

"The one who doubts is like a wave of the sea... That person should not expect to receive anything from the Lord." — James 1:6–7. Doubt destroys what faith can build. Trust must become your daily practice.

Chapter 22: From the Brink to Breakthrough

Ford Taylor wanted to die. He was so tired of fighting a disease that made him want to give up. It was called Lyme disease. Ford shares his powerful story of fighting this disease and how God led him to someone who had an invention that would lead to his breakthrough and even a new transformational product for the medical industry.

Ford Taylor's Journey Through Chronic Lyme Disease

"In 2015, I was in the best shape of my life. My wife, Sandra, even said I was healthier than when we met in our twenties. But within a span of 48 hours, everything changed. I went from feeling vibrant and energetic to dizzy, aching in every joint, and suffering from relentless headaches. Not long after, I boarded a flight to South Africa. The symptoms persisted—and worsened.

When I returned home, I was admitted to the hospital. The doctors initially suspected a carcinoid tumor, but after extensive testing, that was ruled out. Despite months of further scans and bloodwork, the results were inconclusive. Eventually, a much younger physician looked at me and said, "There's nothing wrong with you. I'd trade health reports with you in a heartbeat. Just take antidepressants and oxycontin—you'll be fine."

I wasn't fine.

And I wasn't about to take that advice. Years earlier, I had struggled with suicidal thoughts, so I understood the difference between wanting to die and not wanting to live. Night after night, I lay in bed and prayed, "God, either take me home tonight or heal me and use me to help others. This isn't fair to Sandra."

Eventually, through a friend's referral, I met a specialist who diagnosed me with chronic debilitating Lyme disease. If you ask Sandra how bad it got, she'll say I wasn't just headed for a wheelchair—I was headed to the grave. I'd often collapse in a fetal position. My immune system was so compromised that I picked up every kind of infection. On one occasion, I contracted walking pneumonia and trichinosis at the same time.

In the midst of this, I kept traveling and doing what I believed God called me to do. When people asked why, I simply said, "I'm going to die of something. If this is it, at least I'll die doing what I was created to do."

It was during this time that I received a call from a man connected to a mutual friend. He had heard about my condition and wanted to share his story. A former engineer and scientist, he had once caused a laboratory explosion that left him in a wheelchair. He eventually sought out an obscure technology developed in the 1930s. After just three weeks of using it, he walked out of the clinic. On his way out, he felt God speak to him: "If you'll let me use your engineering brain, I'll show you how to take this to another level to bring healing to leaders I want to use."

When I met with him, he showed me a prototype of what he was working on—primitive, with wires and two-by-fours sticking out—but he had been refining it for four years. He said it wasn't ready for use, but he also believed God had given him something significant.

By late 2018, after another bout of illness and a heartfelt plea from Sandra to focus on my health, I called him again. "Can I be your guinea pig?" I asked.

He agreed to scan me with his new machine, which read bio-rhythmic signals to identify infections like parasites, bacteria, mold, and viruses. After the scan, he looked at me and said, "You're the sickest scan I've ever seen." And he had scanned hundreds.

We began treatments with his high-frequency machine that had never been used at this intensity before. I told him bluntly, "You've got five days. You're either going to kill this disease or kill me."

By Wednesday, I started to feel a change. By Friday, he scanned me again—and cried. "You now have one of the best scans I've ever seen," he said. "Now I know God gave me something special."

Because the original machine was enormous and immobile, he created a travel-sized version just for me. I began using it daily while continuing to travel, and my health improved dramatically. At that point, I invested alongside a friend to further develop the technology—not for profit, but to help others who were suffering with no answers.

We built a more powerful prototype and tested it with various naturopaths and chiropractors, many of whom had been using the older machines in their practices. Encouraged by their results, we engaged professional engineers who believed they could enhance the device even further. They proposed creating a unit four to five times more powerful and capable of running multiple healing frequencies simultaneously.

I sent a simple email to half a dozen consulting clients—CEOs who had seen results with the original device—explaining our goal. I told them there was no business plan, no guarantee, just a chance to be part of something that could potentially bring healing to countless people. Within 48 hours, the full $1.375 million needed for engineering was committed, along with an additional pledge of $750,000 to produce the first 250 units if the prototype worked.

Now, we're in the final testing phase. These new machines are unlike anything we've ever seen—physicists and engineers working with us say there's nothing else like it. I believe God answered my prayer: "Take me or heal me—and use me to help others." And He did both. He brought me back from the brink and gave me a mission far greater than I could have imagined."

Summary

Promise: *"Now to Him who is able to do exceedingly abundantly above all that we ask or think, according to the power that works in us, to Him be glory in the church by Christ Jesus to all generations, forever and ever. Amen." – Ephesians 3:20-21*

Problem: Ford had a life-threatening Lyme disease and did not know where to turn.

Miracle: God led Ford to someone who had an invention that became the tool that would heal Ford and potentially many others through this new invention.

Do You Want to Get Well?

It was just another day in Jerusalem during one of the great Jewish festivals. Pilgrims flooded the city, filling the streets with celebration, prayers, and sacrifice. But just inside the city, near the Sheep Gate, was a very different scene—quiet, desperate, forgotten. A pool called Bethesda sat surrounded by five covered colonnades. And there, day after day, lay the afflicted: the blind, the lame, the paralyzed—waiting. Waiting for a miracle.

A tradition had formed around this pool. It was believed that occasionally, an angel would come and stir the waters, and the first person to step in afterward would be healed. Whether this belief was legend or reality, one thing was certain: hope was pooled there with the water. And hope deferred was also painfully visible in the eyes of the many who never made it in time.

Among them was a man whose body had betrayed him for thirty-eight long years. We're not told his name. We're not even told how he got there. But Jesus knew everything about his condition—both physical and spiritual. And as Jesus walked past the crowds, He stopped for this one man.

With compassion and divine insight, Jesus asked a question that almost sounds absurd:

"Do you want to get well?" - John 5:6

Of course he did—didn't he? But the man's answer wasn't an immediate "yes." Instead, it was filled with hopeless resignation:

"Sir, I have no one to help me into the pool when the water is stirred. While I am trying to get in, someone else goes down ahead of me." - John 5:7

This wasn't just a cry about physical healing. It was the voice of someone who had been passed over, forgotten, and perhaps had stopped believing that change was possible. His focus was still on the method—the water, the angel, the pool—not on the One standing in front of him.

Then Jesus did what only He could do:

"Get up! Pick up your mat and walk." - John 5:8

Immediately—no waiting, no stirring of water, no help from others—the man was healed. Strength surged through muscles long unused. Bones aligned. Nerve endings responded. He stood up, rolled up his mat, and walked.

But the miracle came with controversy.

It was the Sabbath, and the Jewish religious leaders were more concerned that he was breaking their traditions by carrying his mat than celebrating the fact that a 38-year infirmity had just been shattered. When they asked him who had healed him, he couldn't say—Jesus had slipped away into the crowd.

Later, Jesus found the man in the temple. Now healed, the man was in the right place—worshiping. But Jesus had one more word for him:

"See, you are well again. Stop sinning or something worse may happen to you." - John 5:14)

This was no mere physical healing. Jesus had something greater in mind—a full restoration, body and soul.

Reflections from the Pool

This story speaks to anyone who's been stuck—stuck in a condition, stuck in a mindset, stuck in a cycle of waiting. Jesus steps into that place, bypasses the system, and simply asks, "Do you want to get well?"

The man's answer revealed more than a lack of healing—it revealed a lack of hope.

Jesus didn't scold him. He didn't even wait for a perfect confession of faith. He simply gave a command filled with divine power, and a miracle happened.

Summary

Promise: *"He heals the brokenhearted and binds up their wounds."—Psalm 147:3*
"With man this is impossible, but with God all things are possible." —Matthew 19:26

This healing fulfilled God's promise to be a restorer of the broken and a healer of what seems beyond repair. It was a demonstration that God doesn't need methods—He is the method.

Problem: The man had been an invalid for 38 years. He was stuck in a cycle of false hope, unable to access the healing he believed was possible. He was physically paralyzed and spiritually discouraged, isolated, and powerless.

Miracle: Jesus healed him instantly—no angel, no pool, no crowd—just a spoken word. He restored the man's body and initiated a deeper call to spiritual wholeness, pointing him away from his past and toward a future that required repentance and transformation.

Jesus bypassed the traditions, cut through hopelessness, and healed a man who had nearly lost all expectation. That's the kind of promise that starts with a problem—but ends in power.

Chapter 23: "I'm dying."

I turned 70 on July 21, 2022. I didn't realize how difficult that day would be. It seems I subconsciously felt that my life was over at 70. I don't know why. But I always thought 70 years old was ancient. I figured I'd be well retired by that time, and I had made all the money I needed, but it wasn't the case after two failed marriages. That is a good recipe for losing your wealth. I don't recommend it.

I think I had bought into society's lies about aging. In middle-eastern cultures aging is embraced as a very honorable time of life. They called them sages in those cultures. However, in America we have made aging something to be avoided and highly encouraged to use the latest cosmetic treatments to remove every line and wrinkle.

There are some commercials run by an insurance company (Progressive Insurance) that repulse me. They make the idiosyncrasies of a father the object of humor. The message was you want to avoid being like him at all cost. They make him out to be a dufus by the younger generation. How sad we have made aging something to avoid at all cost. Instead, the younger generation could gain so much by learning from those of us in our 70s or older.

Remember the days of old, consider the years of old generations. Ask your father, and he will inform you, your elders, and they will tell you. - Deuteronomy 32:7

The silver-haired head is a crown of glory, if it is found in the way of righteousness. - Proverbs 16:31

It's ironic that society decided that seniors all need a discount. Instead of assuming that seniors lived a successful life that generated wealth and that if anyone should be able to afford something, it should be the senior because he had a successful financial life. Instead, society assumes you're living on Social Security and you need a discount on everything.

I've lost my wealth twice. I was debt-free. But I didn't have enough in retirement to stop working completely. And my wife is still trying to build a financial foundation in her prison ministry.

I genuinely felt my ministry activity was coming to a close, and I had no real passion for doing events, coaching, or even writing.

I began to think about succession planning and considering selling my for-profit company and passing our non-profit to a next generation ministry. I went down that road quite a bit with a few companies.

I told my wife something is not right in my body. I couldn't put my finger on it, I just knew something wasn't right. I had very little appetite and I got winded whenever I did any cardio or just walking up a hill.

I was really struggling with the transition to this winter season. The following year I had a check-up with my heart doctor. I was born with a heart murmur, but it has never given me a problem. Still, I did check-ups every two years.

The doctor wanted me to do an echocardiogram, and then he had me do a stress test because he was a little concerned by what he saw in those tests. The stress test revealed that I had some blockages in my arteries. He wanted me to do a heart catheterization to be able to inspect the arteries by sending up a device up my arm and into the heart area. I went into the hospital fully expecting to return home that afternoon.

My doctor said there are three outcomes of this procedure. Your blockage will be under 70% and you'll go home. Or, it'll be in the 70% area and you will require a stent on your arteries. Or it will be worse than that.

It was much worse than that. I had a 90% blockage in four arteries. They said, "You're not going home. You're going to the hospital for surgery today."

Little did I know how much life was going to change. Two days later I had quadruple bypass surgery. I remained in a hospital for four days and came home. Those four days were the most difficult I've ever experienced. My chest was on fire and I could only breathe about 10% of my capacity. Such a procedure involves opening your chest cavity completely and rerouting arteries from your leg to around your heart.

My daughter sent me this note describing what God showed her during my time in surgery:

> "I heard a still small voice say, 'They did a good job,' as if God was looking over the work the surgery team had done.
>
> A few minutes later I got a text from my dad's wife that all had gone well! And it was not a triple bypass surgery -- it ended up being a quadruple bypass surgery, which is why it took longer than expected.
>
> Two nights after the surgery, I was awoken at 2:30am. I almost felt pain in my chest, but it wasn't like a pain I was experiencing myself. It was excruciating! It was a spiritual burden. I began to pray because I felt like it could be for my dad. It was so intense it brought me to tears. I was awake for a couple of hours with this burden, and then eventually went back to sleep.

> The next morning his wife told the family text message group that he woke up with excruciating pain at 2:30am, but he began to feel like he was getting stronger and was talking better.
>
> I knew God had woken me up to pray."

Over the next five weeks, there was a lot of pain and difficulty walking and sleeping. I entered the hospital at 205 and was now at 183.

I had an open wound on my chest that was not closing and was leaking fluid. At first it was leaking blood and then was later leaking fluid.

I had a check-up with my surgeon to examine my chest and he said I needed to go back in the hospital because the wound was opening up and not healing. There was an infection. Boy was that depressing news!

They decided to do a procedure that made two cavities in my chest into one and cleaned out any infection. It was extremely painful. He said I would have to wear a device that vacuums fluid from the open area until it closed up from the inside out. I went home after three days with this device attached to my chest that had to be attached 24/7.

Over the next weeks, I had to learn how to carry this thing around me with this tube attached to my chest. It pulled small particles of fluid from the chest area to a canister in the device. A nurse had to check on me weekly at home to clean the wound area. That wasn't fun either.

My wife Pamela was an incredible help during this time, and she was an outstanding nurse. She took me back-and-forth to the hospital for check-ups, and I was always looking for ways to improve my situation but it seemed it was never healing. It felt like "Groundhog Day" in my eyes. Every day was the same. It was like watching paint dry every day. I didn't feel like doing any kind of work or ministry activity.

I read my own TGIF devotional around this time and it spoke about age and how God often used leaders in their seventies.

Retirement or New Assignment?

TGIF Today God Is First Volume 2 By Os Hillman

10/29/2023

For a man may do his work with wisdom, knowledge and skill...(Eccl 2:21).

He didn't begin this job until he was sixty-nine years old. He had already had a successful Hollywood movie career and decided to try his hand at politics. He would be known by one job more than any other. He would also be known as one of the United State's greatest statesmen. He had a faith that was genuine but not intruding or very public, but you knew where he stood. He always treated people, even his detractors with grace. He was known for his extraordinary love he had for his wife.

His name was Ronald Reagan, and he did not begin his greatest work until he was sixty-nine years old. By this season of life, most are thinking of retirement in Florida. Ronald Reagan decided to run for President of the United States and successfully served two terms as our 40th President.

It was Reagan's faith that led him to see the Soviet Union as an "evil empire." He'll be remembered as the President who brought down communism in the Soviet Union. And it was his Christian faiththat gave him the quiet confidence and self-certainty that made him a great leader and earned him the title "the great communicator."

Where did he get his spiritual values? There were a number of influences. First and foremost was his mother, Nelle Reagan. I'm confident that had Nelle Reagan died in the winter of 1918-19 - a near-victim of the devastating influenza epidemic that killed millions of healthy, middle-aged mothers around the world

- Ronald Reagan very likely would not have become President. It was Nelle who insisted her boy go to church—a request he happily obliged—and it was in church that Reagan picked up not only those core beliefs and values, but also the intangibles so vital to his success: his confidence, his eternal optimism (which he called a "God-given optimism"), and even his ability to speak. Indeed, history has also overlooked the fact that the Great Communicator found his first audiences in a church. He learned to speak in a church.[1]

Consider this: your greatest work may yet be ahead of you. Don't let age keep you from being used by God.

Retirement or a New Assignment?

TGIF Today God Is First Volume 2 by Os Hillman

10/29/2023

For a man may do his work with wisdom, knowledge and skill…(Eccl 2:21).

He didn't begin this job until he was sixty-nine years old. He had already had a successful Hollywood movie career and decided to try his hand at politics. He would be known by one job more than any other. He would also be known as one of the United State's greatest statesmen. He had a faith that was genuine but not intruding or very public, but you knew where he stood. He always treated people, even his detractors with grace. He was known for his extraordinary love he had for his wife.

His name was Ronald Reagan, and he did not begin his greatest work until he was sixty-nine years old. By this season of life, most are thinking of retirement in Florida. Ronald Reagan decided to run for President of the United States and successfully served two terms as our 40th President.

It was Reagan's faith that led him to see the Soviet Union as an "evil empire." He'll be remembered as the President who brought down communism in the Soviet Union. And it was his Christian faiththat gave him the quiet confidence and self-certainty that made him a great leader and earned him the title "the great communicator."

Where did he get his spiritual values? There were a number of influences. First and foremost was his mother, Nelle Reagan. I'm confident that had Nelle Reagan died in the winter of 1918-19 - a near-victim of the devastating influenza epidemic that killed millions of healthy, middle-aged mothers around the world - Ronald Reagan very likely would not have become President. It was Nelle who insisted her boy go to church—a request he happily obliged—and it was in church that Reagan picked up not only those core beliefs and values, but also the intangibles so vital to his success: his confidence, his eternal optimism (which he called a "God-given optimism"), and even his ability to speak. Indeed, history has also overlooked the fact that the Great Communicator found his first audiences in a church. He learned to speak in a church.[1]

Consider this: your greatest work may yet be ahead of you. Don't let age keep you from being used by God.

Four months later I was completely healed. I had my energy back and began to play golf again. I was still working through the aging thing, but gradually God was giving me a new perspective on that too.

Summary

Promise: "*The thief does not come except to steal, and to kill, and to destroy.* I have come that they may have life, and that they may have it more abundantly." – John 10:10

Problem: I had four blockages of 90% in my arteries.

Miracle: My doctor discovered my problem through a routine visit.

God Heard My Prayer – And Hezekiah's Too

(Based on 2 Kings 20:1–11)

As I lay in the hospital bed preparing for heart surgery, I found myself in a place King Hezekiah once stood: face to face with my mortality.

Hezekiah was a good king, faithful to God. But even the righteous are not immune to life-threatening illness. The prophet Isaiah delivered a message no one wants to hear: "Set your house in order, for you shall die and not recover." It was a death sentence. No appeal. No reprieve. Until Hezekiah turned his face to the wall and cried out to God.

"Remember, Lord, how I have walked before you faithfully and with wholehearted devotion and have done what is good in your eyes." And the Bible says, "Hezekiah wept bitterly."

I know what it's like to pray those kinds of prayers. When the future is uncertain. When your strength fails and all you have left is your hope in God's mercy. Like Hezekiah, I reminded God of His promises. I didn't pray with arrogance—I prayed as a child calling on a loving Father.

And like Hezekiah, I believe God heard my prayer.

Before Isaiah had even left the palace, the Lord sent him back with new instructions: "I have heard your prayer and seen your tears; I will heal you." God not only healed Hezekiah, He added fifteen years to his life and gave a miraculous sign to confirm His word—the sun reversed its course on the dial of Ahaz.

Healing doesn't always come in the form or timing we expect. But sometimes, God moves in power to remind us that He is both the God who numbers our days and the God who can extend them.

During my recovery, I often thought about that sundial. About how God bent time for one man's prayer. It reminds me that our prayers are not lost in the void—they move the heart of God.

My healing, like Hezekiah's, wasn't just about extending life. It was about *revealing the power of God in the middle of a personal crisis*—about glorifying Him in the story that follows. And now I tell it, so others may hope in Him, too.

Summary

Promise: "For I know the thoughts that I think toward you, says the Lord, thoughts of peace and not of evil, *to give you a future and a hope.*" – Jeremiah 29:11

Problem: Isaiah had given a death sentence to Hezekiah.

Miracle: Hezekiah repented and God gave him fifteen more years

Reflection Question

Is there an area in your life right now where you need to "turn your face to the wall" and pour out your heart to God? What would it look like to trust Him completely, even before you see the answer?

Chapter 24: A Swing of Faith - The U.S. Kids Golf Story

In 1991, Dan Van Horn sat on a park bench in Arlington, Virginia, at a crossroads in life. He had just left a ministry role and was seeking God for his next step. In that quiet moment, he heard a word he wasn't expecting: "Golf." Not "kids golf," just "golf."

Dan took that word seriously.

Years earlier, he had been a successful leader in Christian ministry through the Links Fellowship, a Bible study network within the PGA Tour. But now he was unemployed and uncertain of his next move. At the same time, he was a father, coaching his young children in sports like soccer and baseball. That's when he noticed a problem—his kids were struggling to swing standard golf clubs that were too heavy and stiff for their young frames. It was frustrating, not just for them, but for him as a father who wanted to share the game he loved.

Youth golf equipment at the time was a joke—cut-down adult clubs passed off as "junior" gear. These makeshift tools were too long, too heavy, and nearly impossible for a child to use effectively. The result? Discouragement. Kids couldn't get the ball airborne, and the joy of the game was lost before it could begin.

Dan believed God had given him a calling tied to golf, though the full picture wasn't yet clear. He began researching how to make properly fitted clubs for children. Applying physics and common sense, he designed lighter clubheads, shorter shafts, and better grips that were tailored for young golfers. The dream was simple: create equipment that let kids succeed—and smile—on their very first swing.

But designing clubs was one thing. Launching a business was another.

Dan had no job and had exhausted his personal savings. He poured everything into this vision—even his children's college funds. He needed $400,000 to launch, and he hit a wall at $250,000. That's when he turned to God in raw, honest prayer. "Lord," he said, "this is your problem."

A friend helped him produce a simple video explaining the vision. That video reached the right people. Investors—moved more by mission than return—stepped forward, and the funding came through just in time.

In 1997, U.S. Kids Golf was born.

Since then, the company has become the world's leading provider of junior golf clubs. But the miracle didn't stop at equipment. Dan realized that for kids to love golf, they needed to play. So in 2000, he launched a tournament series modeled after the Little League World Series. What began as a 200-player event on Jekyll Island grew into the largest junior golf tournament in the world—now hosted annually in Pinehurst, North Carolina, with over 1,500 players from 60 nations.

And Dan's vision didn't stop there. U.S. Kids Golf created coaching certifications, opened a golf academy, and even purchased a golf course—turning a business into a movement that brings families together.

The Deeper Mission:
Dan never forgot his spiritual roots. At the core, his company wasn't just about golf—it was about family. Golf, he believed, was a vehicle to unite parents and children in meaningful ways. He wanted dads to spend time with their kids, not just on the sidelines, but side by side. And for his employees, Dan

cultivated a culture of balance, integrity, and purpose—a workplace where people were cared for, not just used.

As Dan told me in our interview, "My ministry is to the families that golf brings together—and to the people who work alongside me. That's where I live out my faith."

Summary

The Problem: The golf industry had failed children by giving them tools that weren't designed for their success.

The Promise: God gave Dan a calling—vague at first—but one that would grow clearer with each obedient step.

The Miracle: With no money and no business background, Dan trusted God to bring the right people and resources at the right time. He didn't chase profit—he pursued purpose. And because of that, thousands of children and families have discovered not just a game, but a shared joy that can last a lifetime.

Paul's Race – Purpose, Discipline, and Victory

Centuries before Dan Van Horn took his first swing at reshaping youth golf, the Apostle Paul penned a letter to the believers in Corinth. Drawing from the world of Greek athletics, he wrote:

"Do you not know that in a race all the runners run, but only one gets the prize?
Run in such a way as to get the prize." —1 Corinthians 9:24

Paul wasn't talking about golf or baseball. He was speaking of the Christian life—a journey marked by purpose, self-control, and eternal vision. Like an athlete preparing for the Olympics, Paul understood that finishing well requires focus. It's not enough to start the race. One must train, discipline the body, and press on, even when it's hard.

In the same way Dan designed the right tools to help children run their race in golf, Paul reminds us that God equips us spiritually to run our race of faith. But we must make the decision to run "in such a way" that we actually obtain the prize.

This race is not about beating others—it's about fulfilling your calling. Each of us has a course marked out by God. But too often, we run weighed down by the wrong expectations, poor habits, or the fear of failure. That's why Paul says we must "go into strict training" and "discipline [our] body." He knew that without spiritual conditioning, even the most gifted believer could lose their way.

Summary

The Problem: Many Christians live without intention, wandering instead of running. Like a poorly trained athlete, they are in the race but not striving toward the prize. Without vision and discipline, they drift from purpose—and sometimes disqualify themselves through burnout, compromise, or complacency.

The Promise: Paul offers hope: *You can run to win.* God has given you a race tailored just for you. He's given you spiritual "equipment"—His Word, His Spirit, and the body of Christ.

The prize isn't worldly applause; it's eternal reward and deep fellowship with Jesus. Your life has meaning beyond your current season, pain, or position.

The Miracle: The miracle isn't just finishing the race—it's that God empowers you to run it well. He doesn't just watch from the sidelines; He runs beside you. Every trial becomes training. Every obstacle, an opportunity. And even when we stumble, He picks us up and sets us back on course. Through His grace, ordinary people can finish their race in extraordinary ways.

Final Thought

Whether it's building golf clubs or building a legacy of faith, the race is real—and it's worth running. Dan Van Horn found his lane and stayed the course. So can you.

The question isn't whether you're in the race. The question is: *Are you running in such a way as to win the prize?*

Closing Reflections: The Journey from Problem to Promise

As we bring this book to a close, I invite you to pause and reflect on the divine pattern revealed through Scripture and the stories you've just read. There is a sacred rhythm to the way God works in our lives—a rhythm that often begins not with comfort, but with a challenge.

God's promises frequently begin with a problem. These problems are not signs of God's absence, but invitations into a deeper walk with Him. They are the soil where miracles take root. Time and again, we've seen that when we choose to stand in faith, obey the voice of God, and resist the urge to give up, His power is made manifest in astonishing ways.

But before the promise is fulfilled, there is often a depth-of-soul experience—a time of waiting, wrestling, and refining. This process shapes our character, reveals the motives of our heart, and brings us to a place of total dependence on God. It is in these moments that we come to know God not just as a promise-maker, but as a faithful promise-keeper.

The miracle is never just about us. God answers prayer not only to meet our need, but to bring glory to Himself and to influence the lives of those around us. A delayed answer often leads to a greater impact than an immediate one could have achieved. What may feel like divine silence is often God setting the stage for a greater testimony.

So if you find yourself in a season of waiting or struggle, take heart. You are not forgotten. You are being positioned for purpose. Hold on to the promises of God, listen for His voice, and take the next step of obedience—no matter how small. The problem you face may be the very path to your promise.

Final Thought: Faith Is the Currency of Heaven

Jesus said: *"If you have faith as small as a mustard seed… nothing will be impossible for you."— Matthew 17:20.* Faith does not deny the problem—it overcomes it. Faith doesn't make you immune to adversity—it gives you victory in it. Faith is the bridge that turns your problem into God's promise. The question isn't whether you have problems. The question is: Do you have faith?

What problem has God brought into your life? Today, make a decision to allow God to engage with you to solve the problem. He knows the answer to every problem before it even happens. May you experience His power and grace as you trust Him to create a miracle around your problem.

Your greatest problem may be the birthplace of your greatest promise.

Stand firm. Stay faithful. The miracle is coming.

— Os Hillman

About the Author

A World Leader in the Faith@Work Movement

Os Hillman is an internationally recognized speaker, author, and consultant on the subject of faith at work.

Os formerly owned and operated an ad agency in Atlanta for 12 years. He began Marketplace Leaders in 1995 and since then Os has encouraged thousands of men and women to seek God's calling on their own lives as it relates to their vocation and to view their work as ministry.

Os has written 26 books on faith and work-related subjects and a daily workplace email devotional entitled **TGIF - Today God Is First** that is read in 105 countries today helps men and women fulfill their calling and purpose in their work and life.

Os has spoken in and trained leaders in more than 26 nations around the globe encouraging, equipping and educating people to live out God's calling in their lives. Os Hillman speaks at conferences, churches, luncheons, retreats, and other events and also teaches workshops.

He has been featured on *CNBC, TBN, NBC, The Los Angeles Times, The New York Times, The Associated Press, Newsmax* and many other national media as a spokesperson and contributing editor on faith at work.

Os attended the University of South Carolina and Calvary Chapel Bible School, a ministry of Calvary Chapel of Costa Mesa, California. Os is married to Pamela and is father to his one adult daughter, Charis and son-in-law, Justin. Os and Pamela live in north Atlanta with their three dogs.

Going Deeper!

Join Os for his 8-part teaching series based upon the book.

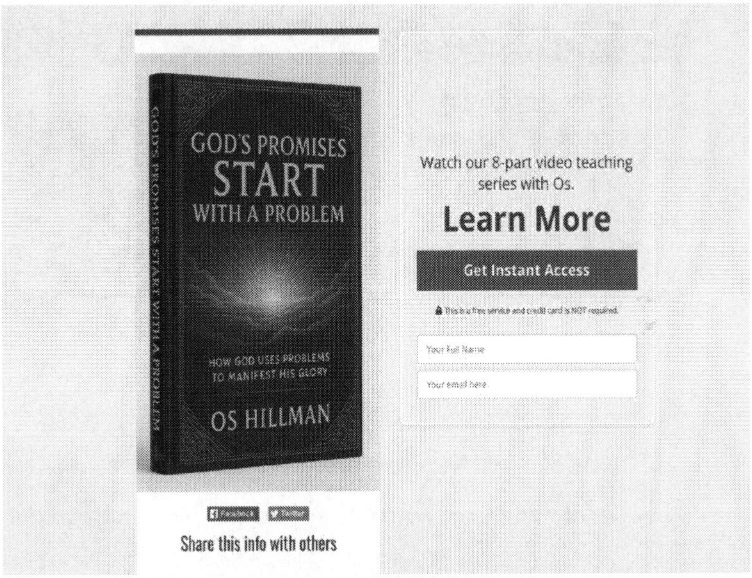

Learn more at www.GodsPromisesStartwithaProblem.com

Ways You Can Engage with Os Personally

TODAY GOD IS FIRST

Daily Workplace Inspiration *by Os Hillman*

Subscribe to Today God Is First – Get encouragement every day by subscribing to our daily devotional, www.TodayGodIsFirst.com

Become God's Change Agent. Mentoring from Os.

Journey to Your Destiny

CHANGE AGENT

MASTER MENTOR PROGRAM

Our online mentoring and training designed to equip you to live out your faith at work.
www.CAMasterMentor.com

Get Inspired by Miracle Stories in the Marketplace

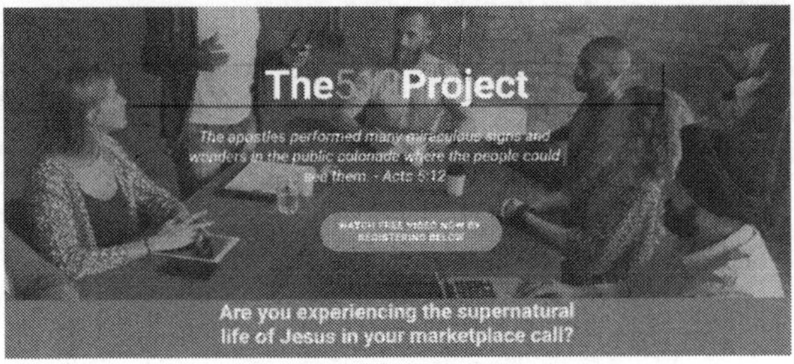

www.The512Project.com

Other Books by Os Hillman

31 Decrees of Blessing for Your Work Life
Birdies, Bogey & Life Lessons from the Game of Golf
Overcoming Hindrances to Fulfill Your Destiny
Listening to the Father's Heart
Experiencing the Fathers Love
Upside of Adversity From the pit to greatness
Change Agent: Engaging your passion to be the one that makes a difference 9 to 5 Window How faith can transform the workplace
Purpose of Money The five purposes for money
Faith @ Work: Do They Mix
Faith@Work Movement What every pastor and church leader should know How to Discover Why God Made Me Booklet
TGIF paper back 270 devotionals by topic
TGIF Pocket Version
TGIF 2 Hardback
TGIF Small Group book
TGIF for Women
TGIF for Men
The Joseph Calling: 6 stages to discover, navigate & fulfill your purpose
The Joseph Calling 12-week Bible study
Proven Strategies for Business Success
So You Want to Write a Book?
Are You a Biblical Worker? Self-assessment

To order: TGIFBookstore.com
678.455.6262 x103 info@marketplaceleaders.org

Want to be mentored by Os Hillman? Check out the Change Agent MasterMentor program at www.CAMasterMentor.com

Want Os to speak to your group? Go to www.MarketplaceLeaders.org and complete speaking request form.

Subscribe to TGIF Today God Is First at

www.TodayGodIsFirst.com

Download our free app TGIF Os Hillman via Google Play or iTunes app store. Search TGIF Os Hillman in your app store

Websites

www.TodayGodIsFirst.com

www.CAMasterMentor.com

www.MarketplaceLeaders.org

www.TGIFBookstore.com

www.The512Project.com

Made in the USA
Columbia, SC
29 June 2025

60032450R00111